Tom Mann's
Social and Economic Writings

TOM MANN'S SOCIAL AND ECONOMIC WRITINGS

A pre-Syndicalist selection
edited and with an Introduction by

JOHN LAURENT

SPOKESMAN

First published in 1988 by:
Spokesman
Bertrand Russell House
Gamble Street
Nottingham, England
Tel. 0602 708318

British Library Cataloguing in Publication Data

Mann, Tom *1856–1941*
  Tom Mann : social and economic
  writings.
  1. Socialism. Theories, 1880–1940
  I. Title   II. Laurent, John
  335'.009'04

  ISBN 0–85124–458–0
  ISBN 0–85124–468–8 Pbk

Photoset, printed and bound in Great Britain by
Redwood Burn Limited, Trowbridge, Wiltshire

Contents

Introduction

Leader with Ben Tillett and John Burns of the London dockers' strike of 1889, secretary of Keir Hardie's Independent Labour Party (1894–6), founder of the Victorian Socialist Party (1906), acknowledged leader of British Syndicalism (1911–14), general secretary of the Amalgamated Engineering Union (1919–21), and a founder of the British Communist Party (1920) – Tom Mann is a familiar name to anyone with the barest knowledge of labour history. For close on fifty years his dynamic personality towered over that of most of his contemporaries in the British labour movement – a period which saw the emergence and firm establishment of Labour as the political alternative to Conservatism in modern Britain. The cottage in which Mann was born (in 1856) and spent the first few years of his life in Foleshill, Warwickshire, is maintained by the Coventry City Council as an important part of British national heritage, and a memorial stands in front of the cottage in Grassington, North Yorkshire, where he died a few weeks short of his eighty-fifth birthday. In Sydney, Australia, the Tom Mann Theatre, an important centre for the arts, is a reminder to Australians of Mann's important place in the labour movement in this country. On 15 April 1936 a red flag flew over the Melbourne Trades Hall to mark Mann's eightieth birthday. Maurice Blackburn, a Victorian Labor MP said at the time: 'Mann it was, who, above all, gave Australasia a socialist and international inspiration'.[1]

But Mann is perhaps less well known today as an important socialist writer, and it is with a view to contributing something towards redressing this situation that the present collection has been put together. Until now, the only examples of his writing that have been fairly readily accessible have been his *Memoirs* (1923; republished 1967 with a Preface by Ken Coates), his

[1] Quoted in Dona Torr, *Tom Mann in Australasia, 1902–1909* (London: Communist Party 'Our History' pamphlet No. 38, 1965), p. 2. (Mann left Melbourne for England in the last week of 1909, but stopped off in Adelaide for a few days in January 1910.)

pamphlet *What a Compulsory 8-Hour Working Day Means to the Workers* (1886; republished 1972 but now long out of print), some short extracts from his long pamphlet *Socialism* reprinted in R. N. Ebbels' *The Australian Labor Movement 1850–1907* (1960), Mann's contributions to the *Industrial Syndicalist* (reprinted 1974 with an Introduction by Geoff Brown) and the pamphlets *The Eight-Hour Day* (originally published as *The Eight-Hour Day by Trade and Local Option*), *Socialism and the Churches* (originally entitled *A Socialist's view of Religion and the Churches* – a shortened, pamphlet version of his chapter 'Preachers and Churches' in *Vox Clamantium* and which is reproduced in the present volume), and *Democracy or Disruption*. All three latter pamphlets were reprinted in the series 'Archives in Trade Union History and Theory' by one of the present co-publishers in the early 1970s.

While the above give some idea of the range of Mann's thought, their somewhat disconnected nature fails to convey an adequate sense of the essential continuity of his intellectual development from his early association with the emergent socialist movement in England in the mid-1880s, through 'new' unionism and political Labourism, to the Syndicalism for which he is probably best known outside of his role in the dockers' strike. The period covered – 1886 to 1909 – was the most fertile in Mann's intellectual output, and the selection of his writings chosen has been done so with the object of indicating the main channels of his thought over this period. Just as Mann was at the forefront of the socialist labour movement of the early to mid-1880s – a movement which arguably brought about the most profound transformation in British politics and society in modern history – so too it was he, perhaps more than any other single individual, who led the workers to the brink of revolution on the eve of World War I. But while labour historians are generally agreed over Mann's importance as an inspiring leader and tireless organiser, too little attention, I believe, has been devoted to his importance as an *intellectual* leader. It is hoped that the present collection will do something towards filling this need.

As mentioned, Mann was born in Foleshill, Warwickshire, in 1856. His father worked as a clerk in a local colliery, and from the age of 10 Mann began working down the mine itself, hauling heavy boxes of coal. After four years of this the Mann family moved to Birmingham and Tom took up an engineering apprenticeship. He had had little formal schooling and so, when the Amalgamated Society of Engineers (the forerunner of the AEU) successfully struck for the 9-hour day in 1871, Mann, at age 15, took the opportunity to begin attending evening technical classes at a mechanics' institute. As he later explained: 'I was one of the kids that was affected by [this change] forty years ago. We started at six and knocked off at six. Then the change came; and instead of averaging sixty hours, it was one hour per night less – making fifty four hours ... As a result of unionist action it was five o'clock regularly. Classes were started, and we youngsters had a chance to attend evening classes. They have been of some advantage, and the important day came for being able to think'.[2]

With his quick intelligence and bent for science Mann soon excelled at these classes (winning, for example, the Queen's Prize for freehand and constructional drawing), which were held under the then Department of Science and Art, South Kensington. He also began making use of whatever free time he could find in the local public library 'giving attention to physiology'[3] and various other scientific subjects. At this time, too, Mann also developed a deep interest in religious matters. His teacher in machine construction and design had been a devout Quaker for whom he retained a lasting admiration, and he also began attending Bible classes at the local Anglican church. From the first though, Mann's independent mind asserted itself, and he was never able to adhere to the forms of conventional religiosity. While later explaining that 'From my childhood I have rejoiced in that religious fervour which overcomes all obstacles', he was not speaking of religion in any orthodox sense. For a time he sought reconciliation of his scientific and religious interests in the writings of Swedenborg, the Swedish geologist/mystic.[4] It was these sorts of influences which later found expression in his chapter 'Preachers and Churches' in Vox Clamantium.

After completing his apprenticeship in 1877 Mann moved to London. There he could find only casual employment, but he did not spend his time idly. He and a few friends 'of a scientific turn of mind' formed a Mutual Improvement Society where members gave talks on such subjects as 'The Chemistry of the Sun', 'Are Other Worlds Inhabitable?', 'Electricity', 'The River

[2] Debate between Tom Mann and Arthur M. Lewis at the Garrick Theatre, Chicago, Illinois, Sunday November 16, 1913 (Chicago: Charles H. Kerr & Co., 1914), p. 61; Industrial Syndicalist, Jan. 1911, p. 36.
[3] Tom Mann, Memoirs (London: MacGibbon & Kee, 1967), p. 10.
[4] Ibid., p. 20.

Thames' and 'The Circulation of the Blood'.[5] Over the next three or four years Mann also began to develop an interest in social issues. He read Malthus' *An Essay on Population* – the book that so profoundly influenced Charles Darwin – but not being content with this author's depressing message he looked further and soon came upon Henry George's recently published *Progress and Poverty*. This book was a revelation. In Mann's words, it gave him just 'what I wanted – a glorious hope for the future of humanity, a firm conviction that the social problem could and would be solved ... it seemed to give an effective answer to Malthus'.[6] The year was 1881; no socialist organisation as yet existed in England, but Mann was already moving clearly in that direction. By 1884 he was lecturing in his old home city Birmingham on Professor Thorold Rogers' *Six Centuries of Work and Wages*, and in 1885 he joined the Battersea branch of H. M. Hyndman's recently founded Socialist Democratic Federation, Britain's first Marxist socialist society. He soon became a regular speaker at SDF meetings, and later that same year he was asked to address the also just formed Fabian Society. It was this lecture which probably served as the basis for his first publication the following year, *What a Compulsory 8-Hour Working Day Means to the Workers*.

Mann sets out in this pamphlet to describe the remarkable increases in production which had been made possible by advances in science and technology – a subject in which he had a keen interest. But he tempers his enthusiasm with a sober evaluation of the benefits to be gained by the *workers* from these improved methods under a capitalist system:

Look again, at the effect of increased scientific knowledge. By a better knowledge of chemistry and metallurgy tons of metal are now extracted from the ore with the labour of fewer men than must formerly have been employed to produce one hundredweight. What I am concerned about is, that in spite of our advanced methods of producing wealth, the workers as a class get only a subsistence wage, whilst an increasing number of them cannot get the barest necessities of life.

Mann was well aware that the increasing 'ease and rapidity of wealth-production ... is of course enriching *someone*', many of whom comprised a class 'of which many perform but little really useful work while the bulk of them serve no function useful in any way to the community'. But quite apart from this

[5] Ibid., p. 19.
[6] Ibid., p. 17.

injustice, Mann was also concerned about what he saw as a lack of rational organisation at the level of the workplace itself, where many people were working long hours (for little return – overtime hourly rates were only marginally above 'normal' rates at this time, and the latter were extraordinarily low anyway) and others were altogether without a job. For this situation, Mann offers a solution: why not share the work around? A reduction in the 'normal' working day (which could be 10 hours or more in some trades) would make more places available for those unemployed, and, at the same time, such a move would have the added advantage of stimulating the economy through restoring purchasing power to thousands. Mann states the argument in straightforward terms:

Let us examine a few figures in order to see clearly how this would affect us. We have something like 7,000,000 adult workers in the British Isles, working nominally under the nine hours system, leaving overtime out of consideration for the moment. Let us see how many more hands would be put in employment if we struck off one hour per day from those in work. It is roughly estimated that of the above mentioned workers there are about 900,000 now out of work, representing a total population of $3^1/_2$ or 4 millions of men, women, and children who cannot get the barest necessaries of life. Now strike off one hour per day from the 6,000,000 in work. The result would be an immediate demand for 750,000 additional workers to keep up production at its present rate, and remembering that these 750,000 would immediately begin to buy more food, clothing, and general comforts, this of course would give an impetus to trade, and so add greatly to the comfort of the entire community.

It might have been objected, of course, that employers would be unlikely to be willing to pay people the same wages for less hours unless output remained at least the same – but that was precisely what improvements in productive techniques had made possible – improved *productivity*, or output per worker. In any case, even without reduced hours, natural justice would seem to demand that increased productivity entitled workers to a greater share in the increased wealth being created, but that this patently was usually *not* the case Mann was also very well aware as he explains elsewhere in the pamphlet: '[O]n every hand a greater result is being shown with less labour. And it must be so else there is no meaning in material progress. But "less labour" means under our existing system . . . not "more leisure", or shorter hours all round, but *less wages*'.

That by this Mann meant less *relative* reward for the employee compared with his or her greater output made possible by technological developments is evident from data which he presented to a Royal Commission on Labour on which he was asked to sit five years later, in 1891. In the interim, Mann gained a considerable reputation as a socialist lecturer (for the SDF), both in London and the North of England, and as a labour organiser. He became a regular contributor to H. H. Champion's *Labour Elector*, and was closely associated with Annie Besant's and Will Thorne's successful campaigns for improved working conditions for the London match girls and gasworkers respectively. By the end of 1889 Mann's was a household name for his part in the great dock strike that year, following which Mann was appointed president of the Dockers' Union. It was in this capacity that he was invited to sit on the Labour Commission.

Mann served on this Commission for two years and gained the respect of co-Commissioners for his assiduous and valued participation in the hearings. One witness at these hearings later recalled: 'His grasp of details, facts and figures is not to be beaten. His information is always ready. He is never befogged ... The shipowner would like to make picketing illegal. Mann follows him up on his own argument and in a few smart thrusts point after point brings him quickly to a helpless standstill'.[7] (Around the same time a San Francisco engineer writing in the *Coast Seaman's Journal* after a visit to England during which he met Mann, Tillett and Burns described Mann as 'a more studious man than the others'.[8]) Returning to the point about productivity then: from data which Mann presented to the Commission in a memorandum on *State Regulation of the Hours of Labour*, and from information supplied by the Fabian Society's Sidney Webb in answer to questions from Mann, it became evident that whereas the total wealth produced in Britain over the previous fifty years had more than doubled (while the population had only grown by about a third), wage-earners had not 'received an equivalent share of [this] increase in productivity ... and many large classes have not had their standard of life raised at all'.[9] To Mann's question, 'Now, could you give me a statement of fact, or an expression of your opinion, as to whether the proportion taken by the

[7] Quoted in Donna Torr, *Tom Mann (with Introduction by Harry Pollitt)* (London: Lawrence & Wishart, 1944), p. 29.
[8] Quoted in *Australian Workman*, 4 Nov. 1894.
[9] Tom Mann, *State Regulation of the Hours of Labour*, in Appendix to *Minutes of Evidence taken before the Royal Commission on Labour*. British Parliamentary Papers, C–7063–IIIA, 1894, pp. 127–30.

wage-earners, as described by yourself now, is greater or less than, say, a generation ago?', Webb answered: 'I think it almost necessarily follows, from the very large increase in rent and the very large increase in the amount of capital upon which interest is paid, that the proportion of the total income which goes in wages is less now than it was 50 years ago, although, of course, it is more in actual amount'.[10] It is interesting to compare this statement with George Dangerfield's assessment of the position of British wage-earners on the eve of the wave of strikes under Mann's and other Syndicalists' leadership in the dying years of the Edwardian era: 'The new financier, the new plutocrat, had little of that sense of responsibility which once had sanctioned the power of England's landed classes . . . [Money] was there to be spent, and to be spent in the most ostentatious manner possible. . . . Society in the last pre-war years grew wildly plutocratic . . . only the workers seemed to be deprived of their share in prosperity; in 1910 the English worker was a poorer man than he was in 1900'.[11]

It was not that the British authorities of 1910 had not had ample warning of the coming revolt. In his 1886 pamphlet Mann quotes the following words from Joseph Cowen MP, speaking at the Newcastle Mechanics' Institute. The labouring class constituted, Cowen said,

a hybrid class doomed to eat the bread of penury and drink the cup of misery. Precarious labour provided them with subsistence for the day, but the slightest interruption threw them destitute. . . . An inscrutable influence seemed to sink them as it elevated those around and above them. Society, ashamed and despairing, swept them, like refuse, into dismal receptacles, where seething in their wretchedness, they constituted at once our weakness and reproach. How to sweeten these receptacles and help their forlorn occupants to help themselves was the problem of the hour. *If society did not settle it, it would in time settle society* (Mann's emphasis).

In his memorandum on state regulation of the hours of labour Mann repeated his warning. The 'meanest labourer', Mann pointedly remarked, is beginning to 'insist upon living a fuller and more complete life than has previously been possible, and it is this desire for a higher and better life that gives the stimulus to most of our modern-day discontent. . . . We have truly a "revolt of labour" in this country'. The knowledge

[10] *Minutes of Evidence taken before the Royal Commission on Labour, Nov. 1892.* British Parliamentary Papers, C–7063–1, 1893, pp. 292–3.

[11] George Dangerfield, *The Strange Death of Liberal England 1910–1914* (New York: Perigee Books, 1980; first published 1935), pp. 218–19.

'possessed by the workers that their power to produce is continually increasing', Mann went on to say, 'supplies them also with the conviction that they are entitled to a greater share of that produce'.[12] The latter point is a constantly recurring theme in Mann's writing, and it is an important one. Mann was no Luddite; he was not opposed to advances in technology. On the contrary, his enthusiasm for science fuelled his belief that science and technology, intelligently applied, held out the surest hope for the material progress of society as a whole. What was required, as he explained a few years later in Melbourne, was 'a revolutionary change in social life commensurate with the industrial revolution', so that 'the ever-increasing advantages of science may be rightfully shared by all.'[13]

In his *8-Hour* pamphlet Mann presents statistics showing the remarkable growth of shipbuilding in Britain and other countries at the time, with all its attendant possibilities of wealth creation and jobs. This was an era of truly revolutionary technological changes in that industry, the steam proportion of total world shipping tonnage growing from just over 12 per cent in 1870 to almost two-thirds in 1900. Shipbuilding and marine engineering generally were also industries in which Mann took a strong personal interest, having worked on some of the latest types of marine engines in London in the early 80s – 'I have rather a hankering after the shipbuilding trade in a way' he explained to the Labour Commission.[14] Shipbuilding, as Eric Hobsbawm points out,[15] is one of those industries where the finished product emerges as a giant single unit, of largely unstandardised materials and with a vast input of the most varied and highest manual skills. It is an industry which requires not only specialisation but also *co-operation*, and this is something which Mann was able to draw to the attention of the Commission.[16] Just as the other commissioners, as well as witnesses, wished to see a reduction in friction between various trades, so did Mann; and the shipbuilding industry was an ideal illustration of the gains to be had for all from greater co-operation and solidarity between unions. Developments in this sphere were already taking place. As Mann was able to

[12] Mann, op. cit. note 9, p. 128.
[13] *Socialist*, 14 July 1906, 30 March 1907.
[14] Op.cit. note 10, p. 241.
[15] Eric Hobsbawm, *Industry and Empire* (Harmondsworth, Middx.: Penguin, 1969), p. 179.
[16] Op. cit. note 10, Oct. 1892, p. 95.

elicit from a Mr. E. W. Bradbrook, Chief Registrar of Friendly Societies, in connection with two shipbuilding trades: '[T]here has been a tendency lately, for instance, among the drillers and hole cutters, for independently registered trades unions to coalesce and form a single one, and withdraw their registry as individual branches'. In fact, as Mann was some years later (1913) pleased to point out in his autobiographical *From Single Tax to Syndicalism*, a Federation of Engineering and Shipbuilding Trades of the United Kingdom, comprising 24 unions had recently (in 1890) been formed, his own ASE being the largest member.[17]

Already, then, we see Mann's consistent endeavours to bring about industry-wide trade union solidarity in action; his later Syndicalism simply represents a logical extension of this principle.

Before the Labour Commission reached the end of its deliberations Mann was already seeking new directions for his energies. In October 1893 readers of *The Times* were startled to read the news, under 'Ecclesiastical Intelligence', that 'Mr. Tom Mann, the well-known Labour leader, is an accepted candidate of Deacon's Orders in the Church of England'. Mann quickly refuted the claim, but did not deny that he had been recently seriously considering entering the Church. In December that year, in an interview published in the *Review of the Churches*, Mann described his attraction to the ethical aspects of religion, explaining that he had for a time earlier in his life, not long after his first arrival in London, been a Sunday school teacher at St. Stephen's Church, Westminster, and had later become closely connected with the Swedenborgian church in Argyle Square, while all the time endeavouring to 'read deeply the works of the Swedish seer, taking also a course of reading in Spencer's *First Principles* and Ruskin'.[18] In a pamphlet which he had written in 1890 with Ben Tillett, Mann had associated this interest in religion with an appeal to some of the older craft unions to overcome their sectional and unco-operative attitude towards 'new' unions like the dockers' and gasworkers': 'Clannishness in trade matters must be superseded by a cosmopolitan spirit, brotherhood must not only be talked of but practised. ... We trust that a real religious fervour will be thrown into the grand work of organising the workers of the

---

[17] Tom Mann, *From Single Tax to Syndicalism* (Walthamstow: Guy Bowman, 1913), p. 23.
[18] The interview was reprinted in the *Review of Reviews*, Jan. 1894, p. 610.

metropolis . . . we call upon all who will, to respond to the call of duty as a religious work'.[19]

It is this spirit which informs 'Preachers and Churches', which was published in May 1894. In this article, Mann defines his understanding of religion as 'those ethical principles that serve as a guide in all matters of conduct – social, political, and industrial alike; and the essence of the whole thing is this: the choice between a life whose actuating motive shall be self, either in acquiring wealth, renown, prestige, or power, and a life which shall have primary regard for the well-being of the community as a whole'. While distinctly Christian Socialist in tone (Mann describes himself as a 'follower of Jesus'), the article does not limit itself to conventional Christian formulae. Thus Mann describes 'salvation' as consisting of 'living in accordance with Divine harmony – in loving order and living it – in hating disorder here on earth, and striving might and main to remove it so that earth may be more like heaven'; and concerning the latter, he writes, quoting Swedenborg: 'Heaven consists of those of all nations who love God supremely, and their neighbours as themselves. Hell is the assembly of the selfish, – of all who love themselves supremely and gratify their lusts at any cost to others'. Yet Mann is at the same time more than happy to quote these lines from the Epistle of St. James: 'Go to now, ye rich men, weep and howl for your miseries that shall come upon you. Your riches are corrupted and your garments are moth-eaten. Your gold and silver is cankered . . . Behold the hire of the labourers who have reaped down your fields, which is of you kept back by fraud, crieth: and the cries of them which have reaped are entered into the ears of the Lord of Sabaoth'. The Hobbs & Co. Liberator 'enormities' to which Mann alludes concern the collapse of a building society the previous year – in which many working people lost their savings – and ensuing revelations of massive fraud and embezzlement on the part of the management.[20]

'Preachers and Churches' is also particularly interesting in another respect, and one which usually receives little, if any, notice in discussions about Mann. I refer to his interest in evolution. This is a recurring theme in much of his speaking and writing from the early '90s onwards. I will return to this subject in dealing with the next reading, and also later on when

[19] Tom Mann and Ben Tillett, *The 'New' Trade Unionism – A Reply to Mr. George Shipton* (London: Green and McAllan, 1890), pp. 15–16.

[20] See *The Times*, 7 Feb. 1893, p. 11.

discussing his pamphlet *Socialism*, but something needs to be said on the subject at this point.

When Mann wrote in this article: 'Democracy is learning how to provide for itself, and never was democracy so truly religious as now. And it is gradually getting more so. This religious evolution will increase as the bad environment is altered on one side, and the ethical gospel is lifted up and followed truthfully on the other', he had more than a figure of speech in mind. Looking ahead for a moment, this becomes evident from a perusal of the first issue of his *Industrial Syndicalist* (July 1910), where he says on page 2: 'The present situation is unique in the history of the World. Never before has there been so extensive a Movement, which, surmounting the barrier of nationality, is consciously striving forward to the next stage in the Evolution of Mankind, where Competition will have to give way to co-operation as surely as primitive Society had to give way to civilisation'.[21] This last quote also provides the clue to what he meant in 'Preachers and Churches'. Mann's concept of socialism stressed the co-operative element, rather than the managerial, and is one reason why he ultimately found himself so at odds with former colleagues like John Burns (who eventually took up Cabinet ministries under Campbell-Bannerman and Asquith) and Beatrice Webb, to whom the 1926 General Strike represented 'the death grasp of that pernicious doctrine of "workers' control" of public affairs through the trade unions, and by the method of direct action ... introduced into British working-class life by Tom Mann'.[22]

For Mann, the co-operative instinct was part and parcel of human nature, but it had been suppressed under an inordinate emphasis on the competitive side of our natures in the prevailing atmosphere of *laissez-faire*. So pervasive had the latter become, as Mann notes in his article, that 'timid Christians and their preachers' were likely to reply that 'to bring about such a change [i.e. to socialism] is impossible; human nature won't admit of it'. What was required, in Mann's estimation, was not only an improvement in the social environment, but also a 'lifting up of the ethical gospel', i.e. a renewed emphasis on co-operation and mutual aid for the common good. As he had argued: what was at issue was a 'choice between a life whose actuating motive shall be self, ... and a life which shall have primary regard for the well-being of the community as a whole'. In another *Review of the Churches*

[21] *Industrial Syndicalist*, July 1910, p. 2.
[22] Quoted in Ken Coates, Preface to Tom Mann's *Memoirs* (op. cit. note 3), p. xii.

interview published shortly after the appearance of *Vox Clamantium* Mann explained: 'Either egoism or altruism must be. We may work for ourselves . . . or we may work for the well-being of our common humanity'.[23] That Mann meant this to be taken in an evolutionary sense is evident in a later article, on 'The Attitude of the Workers in Europe and America', – which he wrote for *Forum* magazine in 1899. 'Cooperation', he wrote, 'seems to be the next stage of human development. . . . The kindly side of human nature is being rapidly developed; and we shall eventually learn to regard poverty as a blot upon our civilisation – as a social disease which must be swiftly eradicated in order that the higher development of the race may be secured'.[24] Mann's final appeal in 'Preachers and Churches' – 'Oh! rich women of the Churches, have you no social and political duty? You, who spend so much on your own persons, have you no care for the *body of society*?' (my emphasis) – also receives added meaning when looked at from this evolutionary perspective. In *First Principles*, Herbert Spencer's volume which Mann explained he had read in earlier years in conjunction with Swedenborg and Ruskin, Spencer, a vehement evolutionist (he, not Darwin, invented the phrase 'survival of the fittest') talks frequently about the 'social organism', or sometimes 'super organism',[25] and this is the phrase which Mann very likely has in mind when he speaks of 'the body of society'. But whereas Spencer, the arch-apostle of *laissez-faire* capitalism and 'Social Darwinism', and almost rabid opponent of socialism (see his *The Man versus the State*, for example) uses the phrase to refer to increasing differentiation of functions and division of labour in modern industrialised societies, Mann clearly means it in the sense of interdependence and commonality of interests – in a word, solidarity. Of course, the metaphor did not originate with Spencer; it is at least as old as the New Testament – St. Paul regarded the Christian Church as consisting of 'many members, yet but one body',[26] and no doubt Mann had this allusion in mind too in his usage of the terminology. It is interesting to notice that in an ILP pamphlet published some years after Mann's article, the writer (T. D. Benson[27]), after

[23] *Review of the Churches*, June 1894, pp. 166–8 (quote at p. 167).
[24] Tom Mann, 'The Attitude of the Workers in Europe and America', *Forum*, Nov. 1899, pp. 325–33 (quote at pp. 332–3).
[25] Herbert Spencer, *First Principles* (London: Williams & Norgate, 5th edit., 1884), ch. xiv.
[26] 1 Corinthians 12.12–13.
[27] T. D. Benson, *Socialism and Service* (Manchester: National Labour Press, n.d.).

starting from the premise that 'all departments of knowledge which deal with social phenomena have their true foundation in the biological sciences', also approvingly quotes St. Paul's use of the metaphor.

Mann's *Vox Clamantium* article was not the first occasion in which he had referred to the evolutionary motif. In 1890, in a letter he wrote as president of the dockers' union to Sydney Holland, he cryptically referred to the need 'on philosophical grounds' to overcome industrial strife 'in order that evolution may not be impeded'.[28] His meaning becomes clear when his conception of 'living in accordance with Divine harmony' is taken into consideration. Similarly, Mann told an audience in Cleckheaton, West Yorkshire, in January 1894 that he 'claimed to be a religious man, as he understood religion' – which was that he 'endeavoured to understand the difference between . . . order and disorder, between harmony and discord'. Mann urged his hearers on this occasion to 'learn to appreciate an ethical basis upon which we should have something like an equitable distribution of the products of labour'.[29] In 1892, when on the Labour Commission, Mann had been asked by fellow Commissioner George Livesey (an industrialist), 'Is not the struggle for existence an essential condition for human happiness?' to which he replied 'I do not want to oppose the argument for the struggle for existence, I am quite willing to take that and even to take the survival of the fittest as an argument. It will not oppose that which I am advocating. I believe the best will be the fittest in good time'.[30] What he meant by the 'best' is apparent from, for example, assurances which he gave to audiences on later occasions that socialism was sure to prevail since it was soundly based in 'our best instincts',[31] and also from an article by Ben Tillett, written in about 1894 (the two worked closely together at the time, but Mann seems to have provided most of the ideas). Tillett wrote: 'We are met very often by superficial people . . . who talk as if they had really read Darwin. But they have not. They talk about the law of selection and the survival of the fittest, without having the least capacity to give a philosophical definition of what survival means, or what fittest means. . . . We have on our side the best intellects . . . we have behind us *the force of the*

---

[28] Tom Mann to the Hon. Sydney Holland, 16 Nov. 1890.
[29] *Yorkshire Factory Times*, 26 Jan. 1894.
[30] Op. cit. note 10, p. 162.
[31] *Socialist*, 1 May 1907.

altruistic principle'.[32] The question remains, *does* Darwin's writing provide grounds for such arguments? This question will be looked at shortly.

In 'Preachers and Churches' Mann claims that 'the whole trend of modern effort in our Trade Unions, Co-operative Societies, Town and County Councils, and Parliament is distinctly socialistic'. These were the heady days of the formation of the Independent Labour Party – the party held its inaugural conference in Bradford in 1893 – and high hopes were held out for it by people in the socialist labour movement. Mann was one of these people at the time; and while many of these hopes remained unfulfilled – many Labour representatives simply siding with Liberal 'reformism' once elected – he never quite lost faith in the possibilities of state socialism obtained through parliamentary procedures. This is easily demonstrated. For example, soon after returning to England from Australia in 1910, full of Syndicalist ideas after his experiences in Broken Hill (see below), he could still write things like: 'at the present hour ... I favour using ALL [Mann's emphasis] effective agencies or weapons at our disposal [for the emancipation of the workers], and I include in these industrial organisation, Parliamentary action and voluntary co-operation'.[33] Or again: '[Our method] shall be Revolutionary ... because it will refuse to enter into any long agreements with the masters, whether with legal or State backing. ... Does this mean that we should become anti-political? Certainly not. Let the politicians do as much as they can, and the chances are that, once there is an economic fighting force in the country, ready to back them up by action, they will actually be able to do what now would be hopeless for them to attempt to do'.[34]

But it is certainly also true that Mann's years in Australia, together with his monitoring of events in Britain over the period (1902–1910), had left him bitterly sceptical about these possibilities. By 1913 he was summing up his state of mind in these words: 'That the Independent Labour Party in its early days was magnificently independent of the orthodox political parties is a certainty; that it is a relatively tame and respectable institution to-day, all will agree'.[35]

In those early days though, things were different. Mann

[32] Ben Tillett, *Environment and Character* (Christchurch, N.Z.: 'Lyttleton Times' Co. Ltd., 1898; originally published by Clarion Press, 1896).
[33] *Justice*, 10 Sept. 1910.
[34] *Industrial Syndicalist*, July 1910, pp. 19–20.
[35] Mann, op. cit. note 17, p. 18.

showed keen interest in the ILP's inaugural conference in Bradford and expressed his wholehearted support from the beginning. Early the following year, i.e. February 1894, he was appointed the party's second full-time secretary. In the meantime, he was asked to stand as the Colne Valley, West Yorkshire, Labour Union's official candidate in the coming (1895) General Election. He did not win, but performed well enough to be regarded as the party's obvious choice when the seat of North Aberdeen fell vacant on the death of the incumbent Liberal member, in early 1896. The contest was to be a straight fight with the Liberal candidate, a Captain Pirie, owner of a local paper mill. After a campaign by the local ILP which Mann later described as 'short, sharp, and vigorous'[36] Pirie was returned, but with a Liberal majority reduced from 3,548 to 430. It was the nearest approach to a win by any ILP candidate up to that time. Mann's campaign speech, *The Socialists' Programme*, published shortly afterwards as a pamphlet and here reproduced for the first time since 1896, is perhaps the best early example of a growing *Internationalist* tone in his writing.

When giving evidence before his colleagues in the Labour Commission (besides seeking information from witnesses Mann also took the opportunity to make his own opinions known) Mann had suggested, in connection with the shipbuilding industry (which was just then experiencing an economic downturn in Britain) that a sharing of labour in such industries on an international scale would be of benefit to all, owners of industry as well as workers. Why not, he suggested, 're-arrange' things so that those sections of the industry which the Americans were best at go to America, and other parts remain in Britain? Mann then went on to extend his argument to cover a wider range of economic activities: 'I would not regret ... that there shall be from time to time a re-arrangement of trades on natural lines according to the capacity of the various countries to produce under the best conditions in those trades. ... [T]here are many commodities which we obtain from other countries which it is not worth our while to make under present conditions, and as long as we continue to devote so much energy to ship building'.[37] In *The Socialists' Programme* Mann elaborates on this argument, and takes in the question of the *social* effects of existing arrangements:

[36] Mann, op. cit. note 3, p. 101.
[37] Op. cit. note 10, pp. 241–2.

[T]he day is rapidly approaching when British commercial supremacy will be seriously questioned and threatened. Nay, not approaching; it has approached, it is right here – I would remind you that the Right Hon. John Morley quite recently referred to the fact – I think on the occasion of his last speech at Newcastle-on-Tyne, that every year brought us intensified competition from every Continental country, and that now we were to be confronted with the competition of Eastern nations. That means, of course, that Japan and China and India are all entering to cater for the world's markets, and therefore British supremacy, industrially speaking, is very seriously questioned. What the orthodox man has propounded is that the British worker shall buckle to, and by one means or another overcome the foreigner, and beat him and drive him to destruction. *I tell you I despise and hate such a doctrine* [my emphasis]. Tell me that the only way for my salvation is, as it were, to drive someone else to starvation and desperation, and I refuse to have salvation on those terms. I for one do not regret that the Continental nations are learning to produce commodities which were formerly produced by Britain, ... I anticipate that Britain must learn to produce more foodstuffs than she has done, because other countries will produce more manufactured commodities than they have done. .... I therefore call for such attention being given to agriculture as shall enable us scientifically to divert the surplus energy from industrial pursuits to food-producing channels. This will bear rigid investigation, it will bear the investigation of scientific experts, and it will bear the investigation and receive the approval of the sound economists of the country.

Mann's position here is in marked contrast to that taken by the famous scientist and 'Darwin's bulldog', T. H. Huxley, at about this time. In February 1888 Huxley published an essay in *The Nineteenth Century* entitled 'The Struggle for Existence in Human Society' in which he says: 'Let us be under no illusions ... we are in reality engaged in an internecine struggle for existence. And however shocking to the moral sense this eternal competition of man against man and of nation against nation may be; however revolting may be the accumulation of misery at the negative pole of society ... this state of things must abide. .... The moral nature in us asks for no more than is compatible with the general good; the non-moral nature proclaims and acts upon that fine old Scottish motto, 'Thou shalt starve ere I want'.[38] Huxley goes on to argue that if Britain is to maintain its industrial lead it must work harder and improve the skills of its workmen through technical education, and 'the rate of wages must be restricted within certain limits'.

[38] T. H. Huxley, 'The Struggle for Existence', *Nineteenth Century*, Feb. 1888 (reprinted in *Evolution and Ethics and Other Essays*, London: Macmillan, 1901, pp. 195–236.

This sort of language has a familiar ring to it in the country where I am writing this – Australia – just now, where we are being constantly bombarded with talk of the need to be more 'competitive' on world markets, etc. Politicians and their economic advisers are so slow to learn, it seems to me, one of the major lessons of history: that the logical extension of such a philosophy is war. In Mann's day it was to be the First World War (which he foresaw – see below); in our day, let us hope it is not something much worse.

Throughout the remainder of the 1890s Mann laboured tirelessly in a bewildering number of capacities. He was on the organising committee of the International Socialist Congress (Second International) in London in July 1896, and early the following year he was president of an International Transport Workers' Conference, also in London. In February 1897 he was giving a series of lectures for the Fabian Society (of which he was a member at the time) on 'Socialism and the Labour Problem', taking as his theme such subjects as 'The Meaning of Ethics', 'Economics and Ethics', and 'Evolutionary Socialists'. In 1897–8 he visited several European countries in connection with his capacity as president of the recently formed International Transport Workers' Federation, addressing numerous large meetings and being expelled from both France and Germany for his troubles. Later in 1898 he took over tenancy of a pub in Long Acre, which became a rendezvous for socialist lectures and meetings. Among the regular visitors were the French emigré communist, Louise Michel, John Morrison Davidson – editor of *Reynold's Weekly* and author of the widely read socialist text, *The Old Order and the New*, and – it is interesting to note in connection with Mann's interest in evolutionary theory – the Russian anarchist Kropotkin, later author of *Mutual Aid: A Factor of Evolution*. No doubt Mann learnt much from Kropotkin, but the influence was not just one-way: in 1907, speaking of the 1889 dockers' strike, Kropotkin wrote in the anarchist journal *Freedom*, 'The strike was a wonderful lesson in many respects. It demonstrated to us the practical possibility of a General Strike'.[39]

For a time Mann was also organising secretary for the National Democratic League, a body which aimed at removing remaining restrictions on working-class voting rights (even by this time – i.e. 1900 – less than thirty per cent of Britain's adult population had the vote), and whose vice-presidents numbered amongst them future prime minister, David Lloyd-George.

[39] Quoted in G. Woodcock and I. Avakumovié, *The Anarchist Prince* (London: T.

Lloyd-George's later efforts in directing Liberal Party policy towards greater welfare objectives can be seen to owe not a little to his association with Mann and other socialists in the League.[40]

In 1901 Mann met a Mr. E. M. Smith, a New Zealand MP, at a lecture given by Smith at the Imperial Institute in London. Mann expressed interest in New Zealand's industrial conditions as described in the lecture (the country had been the first to adopt compulsory arbitration), and also in the country's prospects for economic development (Mann was fascinated by Smith's description of huge 'iron-sand' deposits on the Taranaki coast) and following further discussions, Mann decided to visit the country and see things for himself. He arrived in Wellington in January 1902 and immediately set about contacting local members of the ASE and also a Mr. Edward Tregear, the head of New Zealand's Labour Department, to learn more about the workings of the Conciliation and Arbitration Act. In all Mann spent some nine months in New Zealand during this first visit (he returned for three months in 1908) travelling throughout both islands observing labour conditions and also visiting, as Mr. Smith's guest, the Taranaki district with its iron-sand deposits. (Mann described what he saw as the vast potential of these deposits in an article in *The Nineteenth Century*[41] a couple of years later. Little was done to utilise them at the time however, and this remained the case until very recently. On the television programme *Beyond 2000* last year, I was interested to see that this ore is now being processed and that if current estimates are correct New Zealand should be providing its own steel for at least another 150 years.)

In another *Nineteenth Century* article Mann discussed the efficacy of the Conciliation and Arbitration Act, and it is interesting to compare his views with his later disenchantment with compulsory arbitration. Mann wrote at this time (July 1902):

The workers have made use of the Act very largely; less so the employers. Some dissatisfaction has arisen from time to time on either

V. Boardman & Co., 1950), p. 233.

40 See, Tom Mann, *Why I Joined the National Democratic League* (London: National Democratic League, 1901), I am grateful to Dr. David Howell, in the Department of Economics at the University of Manchester, for directing me to a copy of this rare pamphlet.
41 Tom Mann, 'The Political and Industrial Situation in Australia', *Nineteenth Century*, Vol. LVI (July–Dec. 1904), pp. 475–491. (Mann discussed the iron sand

side, and very strong statements made concerning the operation of the Act and the behaviour of the Court. Only two weeks ago severe criticism was indulged in by delegates at the Wellington Trades and Labour Council, in consequence of the president of the Court having given an interpretation of a previous award in connection with the Wellington painters. I learn that cablegrams were immediately sent to Australia and London, stating that, 'at a Congress of Trade Unionists of Wellington, delegates declared themselves so utterly dissatisfied with the workings of the Conciliation and Arbitration Act, that they would rather revert back to the old conditions of adjusting labour conditions by strike', etc.[42]

From New Zealand Mann sailed to Melbourne, arriving at the end of September. He quickly met representatives from the local Trades Hall and was soon speaking on behalf of Labor (from now on I will use the Australian spelling, i.e. when using the word in its political sense) candidates in the coming Victorian state elections. A few weeks later he was in Sydney, speaking to packed audiences in the Protestant Hall in Redfern, the Balmain Town Hall, and the Sydney Mechanics' School of Arts in Pitt Street. At the Redfern meeting Mann told those present that although 'the power of Britain to produce wealth was never greater than at present', poverty, in absolute terms, was on the increase. Nevertheless, the achievements of rising trade union militancy was beginning to point the way to better conditions: 'The important thing to remember' he explained (in line with the arguments in his *8-Hour* pamphlet) was that 'those who had reduced the working hours and increased the purchasing power of their wages developed a power of efficiency that enabled them to become much more effective workers than they were before. ... Instead of being handicappers of industrial progress, they facilitated it'. Mann went on to declare for socialism and his wish to see installed 'a state of society in which industrial and social harmony would be possible by working on the co-operative basis in the interests of all'.[43]

Returning to Melbourne, Mann shortly afterwards accepted a position as organiser for the Political Labor Council of the Trades Hall – the forerunner of the Labor Party in Victoria – and immediately set about establishing branches in country

deposits on p. 490).

---

[42] Tom Mann, 'Conditions of Labour in New Zealand', *Nineteenth Century*, Vol. LII (July–Dec. 1902), pp. 393–9 (quote at pp. 395–6).
[43] *Worker* (Sydney), 20th December, 1902.

areas where Labor's case had never been heard before. His style was well captured by Labor MP, George Elmslie:

He seems to say to the audience, 'You've got hearts and brains; and I'm going to reach them'. And reach them he does. What a time we have! . . . No mincing or smoodging; no toning down; straight out; the real thing, clear, pointed, and explicit . . . [C]heers for the Labor Party and Tom Mann are heartily given, and those who are favourable to the formation of a branch are asked to stay behind.

Tom does not sit down – before you know where you are he is in the middle of the room planning the rules of the PLC, and taking names down. . . . This is another success; another branch formed, secretary appointed, and night of meeting fixed.[44]

Some idea of the dizzying pace of Mann's activity at this time may be gauged from the following example of his itinerary in western Victoria in June 1903:

1st June	Geelong
2nd June	Geelong
3rd June	Geelong
4th–5th June	Camperdown, Coleraine (PLC Branch formed), Casterton, Branxholme, Hamilton (PLC opened with Frank Anstey), Portland, Terang
6th June	Warrnambool (PLC formed)
7th June	Drove to Hamilton, Port Fairy PLC
13th June	Koroit PLC
14th June	Warrnambool (Town Hall refused, meeting held in Congregational Church).
15th June	Terang PLC formed
16th June	Colac
17th June	Werribee
18th June	Back to Melbourne[45]

When at Werribee, Mann took time out to visit the nearby Melbourne and Metropolitan Board of Works' sewerage farm, and in the first of his two *Nineteenth Century* articles referred to above, he devoted some space to this outstanding example of the applications of modern sanitary and agricultural science: 'This [farmland] formerly carried from one to two sheep per acre. By treating this acreage with sewage, twelve crops of rape

44 Quoted in Humphrey McQueen, 'Victoria', in D. J. Murphy (ed.), *Labor in Politics: The State Labor Parties in Australia 1880–1920* (St. Lucia, Q'ld.: University of Queensland Press, 1975), p. 313.
45 MS itinerary in 'Tom Mann File', Sam Merrifield Collection, La Trobe Library of

and other herbage are obtained per year, maintaining twenty sheep to the acre the year round. The plan is to breed and fatten sheep for the market, and for years in succession some of the very choicest are those from the Werribee Farm'. In all, Mann had nothing but praise for Melbourne's system of sewage disposal – 'that still unsolved problem in London and most other cities in the United Kingdom'[46] – and here again, he displays his remarkable prescience in scientific and technical matters: the Werribee Farm is now being imitated by an increasing number of municipal authorities throughout the world.

But in the area of Labor politics Mann was already beginning to have serious doubts about the value of parliamentary representation. So many Labor members, once elected to State and Commonwealth parliaments, soon became so indistinguishable from their Liberal, 'Protectionist' and 'Free Trade' counterparts as to be virtual defenders of conservative interests. In the same *Nineteenth Century* article, where he noted that, with regard to the recent Commonwealth elections, while 'very few ... of the Labor Candidates *disavowed* Socialism', only a 'minority amongst them clearly and pleasurably declared *in favour* of Socialism; their real attitude being that of Independent Labor candidates, but not necessarily Socialists'.[47]

He remained an organiser with the Victorian PLC until January 1905 (in the meantime – in July–September 1904 – travelling to Western Australia for a whirlwind lecture tour of the goldfields), but he was feeling increasingly more at home with the Social Democratic Party in that State (which had been formed out of the Victorian Socialist League in October 1902, and which modelled itself on H. M. Hyndman's Socialist Democratic Federation in Britain). In socialist journals, such as *Tocsin*, Mann began saying things like: 'The unions are still more effective than any other machinery the workers possess' (*Tocsin*, 8 Dec. 1904), and that too little effort had gone into industrial organisation. Further unquestioning reliance upon parliamentary methods, he now felt, might sap the unions' potential to achieve important gains through more direct modes of action. As one author has noted on Mann's changing attitude here, 'He had not yet lost faith completely in political work. But it was apparent that late in 1904 he had begun to consider again the potential of trade unions for achieving socialism'.[48]

Australiana, State Library of Victoria.

[46] Mann, op. cit. note 41, pp. 489–90.
[47] Ibid., p. 480.
[48] Graham Osborne, *Tom Mann: His Australasian Experience 1902–1910* (Ph.D.

It was in this ambivalent state of mind that Mann began work on his long pamphlet *Socialism*, published in July 1905. (Between March and May of that year he was off on yet another interstate lecturing tour – this time to Queensland where he, characteristically, not only carefully observed labour conditions in that state, but also found time to make a close study of the Queensland government's remarkably well developed system of irrigation from artesian bores.) Mann's continuing *hope*, anyway, that parliamentary politics had a place in the labour movement is evident throughout this pamphlet. Witness, for example, his undisguised pleasure over the recent Labor electoral success in South Australia, where his friend Tom Price, a former stone-cutter (he had introduced Mann to members of the Adelaide Trades and Labor Council, and the two had met on occasion thereafter) had just become Australia's first Labor state premier. Nevertheless, there are definite indications that Mann's disenchantment with parliamentary methods was growing. While rejecting William Lane's efforts to establish a 'New Australia' in Paraguay as impractical and 'Utopian', he nevertheless comes out strikingly in favour of the same underlying philosophies propounded by Lane in the early nineties. His clearest statement is under the heading SOCIALISM AND COMMUNISM:

It is a common thing for some to speak very favourably of Socialism, and very unfavourably of Communism, this arises mainly in consequence of lack of knowledge of what communism is. It is the full realisation of the Collectivist ideal, when not only will the means of wealth production be co-operatively owned by the people, but when there will be no regimentation or any dictatorial official class of the kind we have knowledge of today, when even Parliaments will disappear very largely if not wholly. Socialists desire a free state of society wherein exploitation will be impossible and minus armies of officials or Parliamentarians.

But where Mann differed greatly from visionaries like Lane was in his conception of a 'scientifically' based social philosophy. Engels, of course, had drawn a distinction between 'Socialism: Utopian and Scientific',[49] and in *The Communist Manifesto* he and Marx had likewise distinguished between Utopian and 'Critical' socialism.[50] Mann, however, gives a particular slant to his meaning of the word 'scientific' in this pamphlet, and one

Thesis, Australian National University, 1972), p. 97.

[49] F. Engels, 'Socialism: Utopian and Scientific', in K. Marx and F. Engels, *Selected Works*, Vol. 3 (Moscow: Progress Publishers, 1977), pp. 115–51.

[50] K. Marx and F. Engels, *The Communist Manifesto* (New York: New York Labor

which, in some sense, can be seen as an advance on Engels'
writing. In his Introduction to the English translation of *The
Communist Manifesto* (1892), Engels claims that the concept of
the class struggle 'is destined to do for history what Darwin's
theory has done for biology',[51] but he nowhere specifies the
connection. Nor does Engels help us very much when he
apparently feels it necessary to add a qualifying footnote to his
and Marx's original opening sentence ('The history of all
hitherto existing society is the history of class struggles') to the
effect that recent anthropological studies tended to point to the
existence of 'primitive communism' in *pre*-historic times.[52]
Mann, too, mentions Darwin, along with Huxley, A. R.
Wallace (who had been a co-author with Mann in *Vox
Clamantium*[53]), the geologist Charles Lyell and other scientists
(in July 1905 Mann was lecturing on 'Huxley and Wallace' in
Melbourne's Gaiety Theatre[54]); but he is able to more clearly
spell out the connection he sees between the work of these
scientists and socialism. Mann's concern for a 'scientific'
approach is expressed right from the beginning of his
pamphlet. On page 1 he urges that the 'science of Sociology
should be approached as impartially and deliberately as the
exact sciences, say of Astronomy or Geology'. Such an
approach, in Mann's view, is bound to lead on to an
appreciation of the natural forces underlying historical
development. Just as 'Science has demonstrated that the earth
... and everything that has dwelt upon the earth or that does
now dwell thereon has been and is now subject to the same law
of change or development', so too, do 'Socialists base their
attitude upon the scientific interpretation of history, cheerfully
recognising the universal law of continuous progression'. That
is to say, in history we can see 'a strong confirmation of the
evolutionary theory of human as well as all other
development'. Mann goes on to specify what he means in this
passage:

As in other departments of knowledge, so in Sociological affairs, or the
affairs directly affecting human life. The student knows that the forms
of human society have been such as were necessary for the particular
kind of development at each stage of progress. Naturally some

News Co., 1959), pp. 59–63.

[51] Ibid, p. 6.
[52] Ibid., p. 12.
[53] A. R. Wallace, 'Economic and Social Justice' in A. Reid (ed.), *Vox Clamantium*
    (Melbourne: Melville, Mullen & Slade, 1894), pp. 166–97.
[54] *Age*, 20 July 1905.

sections are mentally and morally in advance of their fellows, and experience the limitations and faultinesses of any given system prior to their fellows, and some of these advocate the desirability of a change, and the kind of change desired is always one that shall admit of humanity developing a few degrees more perfectly than the existing conditions allow of. So in passing through THE TRIBAL STAGE, CHATTEL SLAVERY, and SERFDOM [these are Morrison-Davidson's terms in *The Old Order and the New* – mentioned above], and now in passing through Wagedom or Capitalism, it is found that all civilised society is relatively rapidly getting to think more and more of the community and less of self and ones own family; i.e. not that they become disregardent of the individual and the family, but manifest increasing concern for the welfare of each family and each individual by true concern for the community as a whole.

There are two main points in this passage. The *first* is that Mann apparently believes that in the process of human evolution, a capacity to 'think more and more of the community and less of self' emerges. This is essentially the argument that he had put forward in 'Preachers and Churches', and I mentioned when discussing that writing that the question which naturally arises is whether such a point of view can be regarded as consonant with Darwin. The answer that now can be given is, yes. Immediately above the passage just quoted in *Socialism*, Mann cites Darwin's *Descent of Man*. In a chapter on 'The Development of the Moral Sense' in this volume, Darwin contends that social instincts are important for survival in many species, and have thus probably been preserved and transmitted to later generations through natural selection. Feelings of 'sympathy' and 'affection' for other members of social groupings, and instinctive drives for co-operation in defence, hunting etc. had, in other words, a selective advantage in the 'struggle for existence', and this is why such types of collective behaviour are so commonly found. According to Darwin, 'those communities [of animals] which included the greatest number of the most sympathetic members would flourish best, and rear the greatest number of offspring' – and human beings have probably inherited these same drives. But, Darwin also emphasised the extremely important role of human *reasoning* capacity: 'Although man has no special instincts to tell him *how* to aid his fellow men, he still has the impulse, and with his improved intellectual faculties would naturally be guided in this respect by *reason and experience*'. Moreover, Darwin can see no good reason why, in humans, the operation of these processes need cease at tribal and national borders. In a remarkable passage in this same chapter on 'The Moral Sense', Darwin has these words:

As man advances in civilization, and small tribes are united into larger communities, the simplest reason would tell each individual that he ought to extend his social instincts and sympathies to all the members of the same nation, though personally unknown to him. This point being reached, there is only an artificial barrier to prevent his sympathies extending to the men of all nations and all races.[55]

These kinds of arguments in Darwin, then, can be seen to lie behind Mann's concept of a sense of 'community' and 'common humanity' expressed both in the pamphlet here being considered and in earlier writings. These instincts are as equally part of 'human nature' – in the sense of that which we inherit from our evolutionary past – as is the competitive drive. Unfortunately, this 'kindlier' side of our nature has become suppressed, in Mann's view, under the capitalist ethos; but under socialism, it can once again be allowed full rein, as it had under 'primitive communism'.[56] And as the last quote from Darwin indicates, Mann could also find material in this author conducive to his Internationalist propensities.

The *second* main point that Mann is making in this passage in *Socialism* is that, rather than depending on the principle that 'the simplest reason would tell each individual that he ought to extend his social instincts, etc.', the coming of socialism need not be far away, since 'Naturally some sections are mentally and morally in advance of their fellows, and experience the limitations and faultinesses of any given system prior to their fellows'. Mann is here thus able to ingeniously combine *both* the *revolutionary* arguments of *The Communist Manifesto* (see the section under the heading PROLETARIANS AND COMMUNISTS, where Marx and Engels write about the importance of a more politically aware communist revolutionary vanguard) and more gradualist, *evolutionary* views. As mentioned earlier, Mann had been a member of both the evolutionary Fabian Society in England, as well as

[55] Charles Darwin, *The Descent of Man* (New York: The Modern Library, n.d.; first published 1871), pp. 474, 479, 481, 491–2.

[56] Marx has the following interesting observation in volume 1 of *Capital*: 'Co-operation, such as we find it at the dawn of human development, among races who live by the chase . . . is based, on the one hand, on ownership in common of the means of production, and on the other hand, on the fact, that in those cases, each individual has no more torn himself off from the navel-string of his tribe or community, than each bee has freed itself from the connection with the hive'. See, K. Marx, *Capital*, Vol. 1 (Moscow: Progress Publishers, 1983; first published 1867), p. 316.

Hyndmann's Marxist Socialist Democratic Federation, and both points of view inform his pamphlet. Indeed, George Bernard Shaw's contribution to *Fabian Essays* is cited earlier in the pamphlet, and it is significant that the passage chosen has to deal with the Darwinian phrase, the 'struggle for existence': 'In the earliest days of Socialist advocacy the orthodox political economists pretended to flout as unscientific the contentions of the Socialists; they declared that nature had stipulated we must for ever fight each other on the basis of 'the struggle for existence' – the remorseless extirpation of the weak – the survival of the fittest – in short, natural selection at work. . . . But Socialism now challenges individualism . . . on their own ground of science'. (Actually, immediately under the heading 'The Term, Struggle for Existence' at the beginning of the third chapter of *The Origin of Species*, Darwin writes: 'I should premise that I use this term in a large and metaphorical sense, including *dependence of one being on another*'.[57])

Thus, while Mann's socialism was by this time (1905) moving increasingly towards a more revolutionary, Marxist, stance, this did not necessarily entail a rejection of the Christian Socialism with which he had shown sympathy in earlier years. In an Appendix to the pamphlet headed 'Proposals for a Programme of a Socialist Labor Party of Victoria' (see below), Mann notes:

We are in for a prolonged warfare . . . And yet it is nothing more than the natural evolutionary development and therefore is in the most perfect order. Humanity cannot by any possibility remain in its existing chaotic condition. . . . The Capitalists themselves know this full well, and many, very many I believe, are glad to see signs of the coming change. So with many of those officially connected with the Churches; I know a large number connected with religious denominations, who are sorely grieved at the grossly materialistic conditions that surround them and feel deeply the urgent necessity for a revolutionary change in the basis of human society.

Mann's growing internationalism is also strongly evident in this pamphlet. Towards the end of it he makes a powerful plea for universal solidarity amongst socialists which also shows that, notwithstanding his Christian Socialist sympathies, he was well aware of the role organised religion *can* have in providing 'moral' support for capitalist/imperialist designs:

Socialism enjoins International peace and universal goodwill amongst all peoples. No other influence known to man has operated half so

[57] Charles Darwin, *The Origin of Species* (New York: The Modern Library, n.d.: first published 1859) p. 52.

powerfully to eradicate racial animosities and national jealousies. All through the centuries, led by the dominant class in both countries, the French and English have been slaying each other. Of late years this has given place to incessant industrial warfare; each undermining the other. . . . As Socialists we have no quarrel with the workers of any nation on earth. There is ample room for all in the world, it is only the conducting of industry for the profit-making purposes of the Plutocracy that makes it appear each nation must fight every other nation. Stop this, and begin to produce for use and there is room for all, and work for all and of course a market for all. With us it is not France v Germany, or Europe v America, but each for all and all for each . . .

WE PREACH A PEACE

that so far transcends the peace proclaimed by churches, that whereas the Churches in every nation back up the murderous empire extending policy, Socialists always declare in favour of the solidarity of the interest of the workers of every country.

I alluded above to Mann's proposals for a 'Socialist Labor Party of Victoria', to be established on internationalist principles, and for which he provided a draft programme at the end of his pamphlet. The immediate outcome was the formation of a 'Social Questions Committee' (the name seems to have been suggested by H. H. Champion, who was now in Melbourne editing a literary review, *The Book Lover*) which eventually (in March 1906) changed its name to the Victorian Socialist Party. Even by that time the VSP was not seen by its members – then 758 and growing to over 2,000 in Melbourne alone within two years – as being in electoral opposition to the Labor Party, but rather as a 'ginger-group' for socialism. Throughout this period Mann continued his lecturing in the Gaiety and Bijou theatres and other venues, and it was the response to one of these lectures – on 'The War of the Classes', by the Melbourne *Age* newspaper, that prompted the writing of his next pamphlet, of the same name, which was published in December 1905. This pamphlet is important in marking a distinct shift in Mann's thinking towards a more outrightly revolutionary standpoint.

The lecture, as reported in *The Age*,[58] dealt largely with a recently published book with the same title by the American author Jack London. With reference to London's claim that there were 10 million unemployed in the United States and that 'there was continual warfare between the working classes and the great trusts', Mann had declared that 'The same war of the

[58] *Age*, 27 Nov. 1905.

classes that was taking place in America was in progress in Australia, and would continue as long as the present capitalist system continued'. Mann was also reported to have said 'Had there been no America and no Australia there would have been a revolution in England before this. It had been a curse for the English people that there had been an America and an Australia . . . The direct cause – there were other causes as well – of the engineering of the South African War was the necessity of finding another outlet for the young and energetic men of England'. The question that naturally occurs to one is whether Mann's lecture was fairly reported in the first place, but since Mann does not take issue with the *Age* editor on this point we can presumably take it that the quoted lines do represent some approximation to his phraseology. But what clearly *was* lacking, as we can see from Mann's reply, was a fair account of the full context in which Mann used these phrases. Anyone who doubts the accuracy of what Mann had to say when he wrote 'The capitalists are shrewd enough to know that an outlet for such [i.e. discontented] young men must be afforded, or internal social revolt will receive attention', and 'Empires exist not in the true interests of the whole people, but to enable a class to perpetuate its domination', need only turn to these revealing lines published some years later (in 1917) in Lenin's *Imperialism, the Highest Stage of Capitalism*:

Cecil Rhodes, we are informed by his intimate friend, the journalist Stead, expressed his imperialist views to him in 1895 in the following terms: 'I was in the East End of London yesterday and attending a meeting of the unemployed. I listened to the wild speeches, which were just a cry for 'bread! bread!' and on my way home I pondered over the scene and I became more than ever convinced of the importance of imperialism . . . My cherished idea is a solution for the social problem, i.e., in order to save the 40,000,000 inhabitants of the United Kingdom from a bloody civil war, we colonial statesmen must acquire new lands to settle the surplus population, to provide new markets for the goods produced in the factories and mines. The empire, as I have always said, is a bread and butter question. If you want to avoid civil war, you must become imperialists.[59]

As to the *Age* editor's assertion that 'the very phrase, "The War of the Classes" . . . is borrowed from the early German Socialism', Mann points out that his lecture was about Jack London's book – which is not mentioned anywhere in the *Age* article – not about 'the kind of Socialism which he [Mann]

59 V. I. Lenin, *Imperialism, the Highest Stage of Capitalism* (Moscow: Progress Pub-

might have heard when he was a small boy in London in the parks on Sunday afternoon'. (In fact, there was very little socialism being preached in London in the 1860s, when Mann was a 'small boy'. After the decline of Chartism in the late 1840s, socialism did not re-emerge in Britain until the early to mid-1880s, at which time, as noted, Mann was at the forefront of the movement.)

Finally, it is interesting to notice the apparent growing currency of the terms 'evolutionary' and 'revolutionary' among socialists at this time. Mann, as we have seen, had been interested in evolution from the early 1870s, and he had been using the term in the context of labour politics from at least 1890, so the *Age* editor's claim that Mann was behind the times in his advocacy of revolutionary views does not stand up. Mann had been anticipating much of the sort of discussion on the place of 'evolution' and 'revolution' in socialist circles that the *Age* editor refers to (as, for instance, in Bernstein's *Evolutionary Socialism*), and was already moving beyond this. As can be seen, his quotation from Hyndman's *Economics of Socialism* is substantially in line with his own arguments in *Socialism*. It might also be mentioned that London's volume, too, contains much discussion centred on the evolution theme,[60] a word which was much bandied about in the early years of this century when 'Social Darwinists' of the John D. Rockefeller stamp were saying things like (in a Sunday school address): 'The growth of a large business is merely a survival of the fittest . . . It is merely the working out of a law of nature and a law of God'.[61] The question of whether Mann's socialism was 'evolutionary' or 'revolutionary' was also taken up by Tom's wife, Elsie Mann, in an article she wrote in the first issue of the Melbourne *Socialist* (see shortly) in April 1906:

To call oneself an evolutionary Socialist, as distinct from a revolutionary Socialist, means nothing at all beyond an endorsement of the application of the evolutionary theory of Socialism, which was admitted by Herbert Spencer, who, through miscomprehension, hated and abhorred Socialism. To be logical it is necessary to be revolutionary, as believing in and working for a complete change in social conditions. All revolutionary Socialists are evolutionary Socialists. Marx and Engels were revolutionary Socialists, and were the

lishers, 1983; first published 1917), p. 75.

[60] See, especially, the essay 'Wanted: A New Law of Development' in this volume.

[61] Cited in, R. Hofstadter, *Social Darwinism in American Thought* (Boston, Mass.:

first to express the theory of social evolution, as stated in their 'Communist Manifesto', published in 1848. Knowing the tendency of events by a scientific study of history and economics, the Socialist can watch the evolutionary processes, and aid towards their completion, i.e., the revolution he so ardently hopes for, and which a class-conscious people alone will be able to direct and guide in their best interest.[62]

Mann's lecturing for the VSP continued apace from early 1906, at the old venues and in new ones like Melbourne's Guild Hall, in subjects as widely ranging as 'Swedenborg and his Teachings', 'Evolution in Nature, Industrialism, and Politics', 'Man's Place in Nature' (the title of a much discussed book by T. H. Huxley), 'Various Stories of Creation', 'Scandinavian Mythology', 'The Religion of Social Democracy', 'Evolution and the Churches', 'The Wonders of Science', 'Recent Developments in Machinery and Science', 'The Evolution of Man', and 'Communism amongst Animals'.[63] Mann was also involved in the establishment of a Socialist Institute in Melbourne, along the lines of a mechanics' institute, and of which he was secretary. Among occasional lecturers at the latter were Professors Skeats and Osborne from Melbourne University, professors of geology and physiology respectively. A new official journal for the VSP, *The Socialist*, was started on 2nd April 1906 with Mann as editor, and soon became a weekly. Among its regular contributors were the radical Victorian Labor MPs Harry Scott Bennett and Frank Anstey, the noted poet Bernard O'Dowd, Miss Amelia Lambrick (who wrote under the name 'Hypatia', after the Alexandrian philosopher heroine in Charles Kingsley's novel), and future Labor Prime Minister John ('Jack') Curtin. Organising work continued throughout Victoria over the next couple of years, with Mann travelling to outlying towns like Euroa, Monbulk (a fruit growing district, where he spoke in support of efforts to set up a co-operative cannery), and Ferny Creek. In June and July 1907 he was again in Sydney – with Ben Tillett, who was currently visiting Australia, in support of a coal lumpers' strike – following which he made a short visit to the 'Silver City' in far western NSW, Broken Hill. The latter city was to be the scene of Mann's final conversion to militant direct action, in the Syndicalist sense, in 1908–9. In the meantime, between April

Beacon Press, 1955), p. 45.

[62] *Socialist*, 2 April 1906.
[63] *Socialist*, 19 May, 8 Sept., 1 Oct. 1906; 2 Feb.; 1, 4 May; 14 Sept., 1 Oct. 1907.

and June 1908, as mentioned earlier, Mann made a second visit to New Zealand.

As a two year agreement between the unions and the largest mining company in Broken Hill, the Broken Hill Proprietry Co. (BHP) drew to a close towards the end of 1908, word got around that the company intended reducing wages to 1906 levels, a cut of 12.5 per cent. In September, 1908 the local branch of the Amalgamated Miners' Association (AMA), therefore, offered Mann a position as paid organiser for this union and others on the Barrier in anticipation of a major confrontation. Mann accepted, and within three weeks of his arrival in Broken Hill shortly afterwards had augmented the AMA's membership by 1,600.[64] By January 1909 the situation had crystallised. The miners went on strike, and in response BHP discharged all employees except the watchmen, and were joined in the move by the Block 10 and British mining companies. Meanwhile, 350 police had arrived in the city. On 9th January the police, wielding batons, broke up an afternoon picket march of approximately 1,000 men led by Mann and other union leaders, and 27 marchers, including Mann, were arrested. George Dale, writing a few years afterwards, has left a memorable picture of the incident:

As usual, the four o'clock shift left the Trades Hall, with Tom Mann leading the band. The first place the pickets were to be relieved at was at the corner of Crystal Lane and Sulphide Street. Being Saturday afternoon there was a large number of people in the street, amongst whom were numerous police, as distinguished by their white helmets. When approaching the boundary line of the company's lease a voice called 'halt!' However, as the order did not come from Tom Mann those marching took no heed, as they had but a few more paces to go before reaching their usual halting-place. Then . . .

In a trice all was confusion, consternation, disorder, violence – men (and women, too) were being batoned in all directions. Tom Mann was struggling with at least fifteen policemen. Arrests were being made in all directions. Police, in the excitement, were flourishing revolvers in one hand and striking with batons with the other . . .[65]

This action incensed the city. Thousands of men and women – 15,000 on one occasion – marched in protest processions, and while Mann was bailed out on condition that he refrained from

[64] See, 'Forcing a Strike', in Barrier Daily Truth, special centenary (of Broken Hill) edition, 1983.
[65] George Dale, The Industrial History of Broken Hill (Melbourne: Fraser & Jenkinson, 1918), p. 117.

speaking publicly in New South Wales, this did not prevent huge crowds turning out to hear him – up to 3,000 supporters at a time took a special 'Tom Mann Train' (which required two engines to haul it) to Cockburn, just over the border in South Australia, to hear him speak there. The *Barrier Miner* newspaper wrote of these occasions: 'It was evident that if Mr. Mann could not go to Broken Hill to advocate his views then Broken Hill in its thousands would go to Mr. Mann'.[66]

The strike continued for 21 weeks in both Broken Hill and Port Pirie (where the company's smelters were situated), being one of the longest in Australian labour history. Mann was committed for trial in Albury on charges of sedition and incitement to riot, but was acquitted, and returned to a hero's welcome in Broken Hill in early May. Meanwhile the unions had, to all appearances, won – BHP agreed to maintain guaranteed contracts at the current levels of wages after a decision in the unions' favour handed down by Mr. Justice Higgins of the Arbitration Court. However, any elation was to be short-lived. BHP appealed against the decision to the High Court, which body upheld the Higgins Award except for the clauses relating to the contract system and working days, which it found beyond its jurisdiction. The men remained out until May 23 but BHP were in no hurry to open its mine – many starving miners were forced to leave the city to seek work elsewhere.

In these bitter circumstances Mann wrote his pamphlet, *The Way to Win*, which was first published in the AMA's own daily, the *Barrier Daily Truth*, in May 1909, and reprinted as a pamphlet shortly afterwards. The first sentence of this pamphlet immediately indicates just how far Mann was now prepared to go in the direction of thoroughgoing Syndicalism: 'The great crisis is drawing nigh when the supreme effort must be made by the workers to *take entire responsibility for the management of all industry and commerce*; the existing system of society must of necessity give place to some other system that will adequately provide for the requirements of all'. To achieve this, he goes on to say, THE PRELIMINARY ESSENTIAL CONDITION IS WORKING-CLASS SOLIDARITY, without which 'the power and the disposition to act in concert as the working class against the dominating plutocratic class' is doomed to failure. The next sentence, though, is more problematic, and shows Mann's continuing reluctance to altogether dismiss the possibility of some gains to be made in

[66] Quoted in Edward Stokes, *United We Stand: Impressions of Broken Hill 1908–1910*

the political sphere: 'At present we have not got this solidarity, either industrially *or politically* [my emphasis]'. Indeed, further on in the pamphlet he states explicitly: 'I am not wishful to deprecate political action', and later: 'I am not an anti-Parliamentarian'.

In October the previous year, just after he had taken up the job of organiser for the AMA, Mann had actually become involved in a disagreement over this issue with Bob Ross and Harry Holland from the local 'Barrier Socialist Group' of the Socialist Federation of Australia (SFA) at a welcoming social for Mann at the Trades Hall. Ross and Holland, the *Barrier Daily Truth* had noted, 'differed from Mr. Mann as to the attitude of the SFA to members of the Labor Party'.[67] As already indicated, Mann was not to change his attitude noticeably in this respect in his espousal of syndicalism on arrival back in England. It is also interesting to notice Mann's insistence that 'workers should get their education in industrial and social economics, and this would prove the true guide to political action'.

Nevertheless, the tone of the pamphlet is clear enough: it represents a major departure in Mann's thinking to a preoccupation with what he calls 'industrial unionism', the breaking down of remaining divisions in the union movement. He presents his case cogently in these lines:

The weakness of our industrial organisation lies less in the fact that only one-fourth of the workers are organised, than in the much more serious fact that those who are organised are not prepared to take common cause with each other.

Hitherto we have been content with trades unions – meaning unions of skilled workers, supplemented by unions of unskilled workers. But each of these unions has for the most part initiated and as far as possible carried out a policy for itself alone . . . [T]he basis of unionism today is distinctly sectional and narrow, instead of cosmopolitan and broad-based.

The first paragraph in this quotation no doubt partly reflects Mann's disgust over the recent activities of some unionists in connection with the strike. He later described these actions in his *Memoirs*:

[T]he armed police and other henchmen of the companies were transported from Sydney to Broken Hill by the instrumentality of the organized railwaymen of New South Wales. At Albury, the police, etc., were handed over to the care of the organized railwaymen of the

(Canterbury, Vic.: Five Mile Press, 1983), p. 189.

[67] *Barrier Daily Truth*, 16 Oct. 1908.

State of Victoria. These latter took them to the boundary of the next State, where again the forces hostile to the working class, were handed over to the organized railwaymen of South Australia. These railwaymen were practically all union men, who nevertheless lent themselves to the fighting of the battles of the master class against the working class! Yet they were in full sympathy with the Broken Hill men, and were actually subscribing funds to help the miners in the fight. In their daily labour, however, they not only frustrated all they had done by friendly letters and subscriptions, but took charge of, fed, and carried the persons, ammunition, horses, etc., etc., to the scene of action, thus enabling the master class to have at its disposal the machinery of the State and the services of the organized workmen to beat the miners.[68]

It followed too, of course, that Mann's disillusionment with compulsory arbitration was by now complete. He expresses this loss of faith in a system which had once attracted him to New Zealand in the first place in this pamphlet; and he later touched on the subject again in the *Industrial Syndicalist*:

Not very long ago I was at a place called Broken Hill, in New South Wales. There was the Industrial Dispute Act of the State and there is a Federal Arbitration Act covering a dispute when it extends over the boundaries of more than one state. They resorted to this machinery. The workers said they were desirous of having the difficulty closed before there should be another stoppage. They did not want to stop. The Arbitration Act is there in order to prevent industrial disputes, but it could not stop the bosses from locking-out. And they did lock out in spite of the Act, because no Act has ever been framed that, under the capitalist system, is going to take away the right of the employer who refuses to keep his works open. None of the Arbitration Acts take away the power of the employer to lock-out, though they take away the power of the worker to strike.[69]

Finally, Mann's Internationalism has by now reached full maturity. He is pleased to note developments in France, Germany and Italy substantially in line with his own way of thinking. (Soon after returning to England in May 1910 Mann travelled to Paris with the journalist Guy Bowman, translator of Gustave Hervé's anti-militarist classic *My Country Right or Wrong*, to learn of the latest developments in French Syndicalist thinking.) He notes in *The Way to Win* that 'On all sides we see hysterical developments being made by the plutocratic Governments of the different countries to prepare for war on an unprecedented scale, as a relief from glutted markets'. The only possible hope for averting disaster, in Mann's view, was

[68] Mann, op. cit. note 3, p. 193.
[69] *Industrial Syndicalist*, Jan. 1911, pp. 48–9.

the international solidarity of the workers: 'Sectionalism must disappear, and the industrial organisations must be equal to State, national, and international action, not in theory only, but in actual fact'. As he had expressed it a few months earlier in Melbourne:

Our comrades realise that they are members of a world-wide Brotherhood and Sisterhood. No narrow nationalism can satisfy our people. Nothing short of Cosmopolitanism can really satisfy a world citizen. 'The world is my country!' is the declaration of every Socialist. It is our mission then to speed the day when racial antipathies shall be completely obliterated, when national boundaries will exist only as indicating that certain areas were the cradles of certain peoples. But no longer will the tax gatherer be ready to pounce upon the traveller; no more shall soldiery be wasting their days tramping up and down in defence of a plutocracy; the requirements of all people will be supplied; identity of interests will again be understood and acted upon, and the people will be economically free, intellectually alert and morally strong to live the allotted span under healthy and lovable conditions, all reasonably sharing in the joys of healthy life.[70]

It is a pity not more people could have thought this way in 1914.

---

[70] *Socialist*, 31 July 1908.

Acknowledgements

I am grateful to Ken Coates and Ken Fleet of SPOKESMAN books, and to George Campbell, National Secretary of the Amalgamated Metal Workers' Union (of Australia) for their encouragement and support in getting this book together; and also to Peter Cochrane, Peter Sheldon, Jim Hagan, Ian Inkster, Roy MacLeod and Randall Albury for helpful discussions. Most of all, I am grateful to Tom Mann for the pleasure and inspiration his writing has given me.

Department of Economic History
University of New South Wales
June 1987   JOHN LAURENT

CHAPTER ONE

What a Compulsory 8-Hour Working Day Means to the Workers*

Oh Slaves of these laborious years,
Oh Freemen of the years to be:
Shake off your blind and foolish fears,
And hail the Truth that makes you free.

The appalling amount of distress that exists in every town in Britain must arrest the attention of all duty loving men and women. No one who sees the effects of want and the fear of want can passively behold the dire poverty of a large section of the workers. Rather will he probe and probe until he finds the cause of the disease. Socialists *have* probed and they find the disease of want to be spread by the profit-making system upon which all industry and society itself is based. They know that five or six centuries ago, without machinery, Englishmen obtained for their work sufficient to keep them in vigorous health and that they were not subject to periodical trade depressions; and when they further reflect upon the fact that the working day then consisted of no more than eight** hours, no wonder that socialists are discontented with the present state of affairs, and that they resolve to use every means in their power to replace the present discord, misery, and anarchy, with harmony, happiness, and order.

The effect of our so-called labour-saving machinery (used really by its owners to save *wages* and not *labour*) is to cause continual distress amongst the workers by mercilessly throwing them out of employment without any compensation. It may then take a man often months, sometimes years, to find an occupation of any kind and when found it is at a price much below that he was in receipt of before the machine disturbed him. Yet the machine has increased the ease and rapidity of wealth-production. This increase of wealth is of course enriching *someone* – a class of which many perform but little really useful work while the bulk of them serve no function

* First published by The Modern Press, London, 1886.
** See *Work and Wages* by Thorold Rogers, MP.

useful in any way to the community. Look, again, at the effect of increased scientific knowledge. By a better knowledge of chemistry and metallurgy tons of metal are now extracted from the ore with the labour of fewer men than must formerly have been employed to produce one hundredweight. What I am concerned about is, that in spite of our advanced methods of producing wealth, the workers as a class get only a subsistence wage, whilst an increasing number of them cannot get the barest necessaries of life.

Optimist politicians are unwilling to admit that this is so. Anxious to make out a good case for the present basis of society, they ignore the plainest of facts, so in confirmation of my contention I will quote from one or two non-socialists. Professor Thorold Rogers, the present MP for Bermondsey, says on pages 185–6 of 'Six Centuries of Work and Wages', written in 1884.

It may be well the case, and there is every reason to fear it is the case, that there is collected a population in our great towns which equals in extent the whole of those who lived in England and Wales six centuries ago; but whose condition is more destitute, whose homes are more squalid, whose means are more uncertain, whose prospects are more hopeless than those of the poorest serfs of the Middle Ages and the meanest drudges of the mediaeval cities. The arm of the law is strong enough to keep them under, and society has no reason to fear their despair; but I refuse to accept the superficial answer that a man is an admirer of the good old times because he insists that the vaunts of civilisation should be examined along with, and not apart from its failures. It is not possible to give the solution of one problem, the growth of opulence, and to refuse all attention to the other problem, the growth of penury.

Joseph Cowen MP speaking at a Mechanics' Institute at Newcastle, alluded to the labouring section as 'a hybrid class doomed to eat the bread of penury and drink the cup of misery. Precarious labour provided them with subsistence for the day, but the slightest interruption threw them destitute. A week of broken weather brought thousands of these industrial nomads to the brink of starvation. An inscrutable influence seemed to sink them as it elevated those around and above them. Society, ashamed and despairing, swept them, like refuse, into dismal receptacles, where seething in their wretchedness, they constituted at once our weakness and reproach. How to sweeten these receptacles and help their forlorn occupants to help themselves was the problem of the hour. *If society did not settle it, it would in time settle society.*'

To this socialists answer that there is no permanent way of sweetening the lives of the class referred to except by the complete annihilation of the profit-mongers as a class, by forcing them all into the ranks of the *useful* workers. This will be apparent when it is realised that under the present system we are working to supply profits to profit-mongers instead of working to supply the legitimate requirements of the entire community, and when it is borne in mind that shareholders and employers are contented with nothing less than the *highest* possible profits, it will also be seen that on the other hand we (the workers) can have nothing more than the *lowest* possible wages. To establish society on a proper basis is therefore the work of every right-minded man or woman.

Demagogues have been at work – with good intentions perhaps – but they have misled the workers from the true cause of their troubles. Among the blind leaders of the blind may be mentioned the Malthusians, the Teetotallers, the Financial Reformers, and well-intentioned Radicals. The first mentioned have taught that there are too many people in the country, and that the only way of bettering our condition is by curtailing the population, and this in face of the fact that every year wealth in this country is increasing much faster than population. The Temperance advocates hammer away at the blessings of sobriety as though drunkenness was the cause of poverty, when the fact is the other way about. Well nigh as fast as they surround an old toper with influences that prevent his drinking tastes being gratified, another fills up the hole out of which he was lifted. It is a useless expenditure of energy to be continually preaching temperance and thrift. Let all be blest with leisure, food and healthy enjoyments, as they might be if the economic basis of society was as it should be, and then these matters will all right themselves. The only reason people spend time upon these panaceas is because they fail to understand the law of wages, which is that all above a bare subsistence wage shall go to profit-mongers as profit. The only way out is to *destroy the profit-mongers*.

The same argument applies to the financial reformer. All sensible persons are of course agreed that the country should be governed as economically as is consistent with efficiency, as also all are agreed that we should live soberly. But the reformer fails to see that if we curtail taxation to its lowest possible minimum, reduce it if you will 90 per cent, not one farthing of it would be saved to the workers. The Iron Law would still be in force which says, 'So much as will keep life in you *and no more* shall go to you, O ye workers, so long as the profit making system remains.'

These economic questions cannot be understood in a sufficiently clear manner by the mass of the workers while they are absorbed twelve, fourteen, sixteen, and even more hours a day while in work, and when out of work are walking about with the pangs of hunger eating out their vitals, and the blackness of despair staring them in the face at every turn. Now suppose those of us who can see these things in something like their grim reality, decide that come what may, we at least will do our part towards obtaining remunerative employment for all, and at the same time sufficient leisure that all may have a little breathing time after their work, what course can we take? To this I reply, there is one way by which it can be done, viz, by at once concentrating our efforts towards the establishing of an eight hours working day.

Let us examine a few figures in order to see clearly how this would affect us. We have something like 7,000,000 adult workers in the British Isles, working nominally under the nine hours system, leaving overtime out of consideration for the moment. Let us see how many more hands would be put in employment if we struck off one hour per day from those in work. It is roughly estimated that of the above mentioned workers there are about 900,000 now out of work, representing a total population of $3\frac{1}{2}$ or 4 millions of men, women, and children who cannot get the barest necessaries of life. Now strike off one hour per day from the 6,000,000 in work. The result would be an immediate demand for 750,000 additional workers to keep up production at its present rate, and remembering that these 750,000 would immediately begin to buy more food, clothing, and general comforts, this of course would give an impetus to trade, and so add greatly to the comfort of the entire community for a year or two. These advantages, however, would soon be swallowed up by fresh displacements of labour due to more efficient machinery and advancing scientific knowledge; but, during the year or two that it gave relief, see how immensely it would add to the leisure and therefore to the general intelligence of the workers. And increased intelligence means more active discontent with our conditions of life, and in due course a hastening of the overthrow of the present capitalistic domination.

I am fully aware that there are some who claim to have a knowledge of workers who contend that the very success of an Eight Hours Movement would simply mean a perpetuation of

the present wretched system, as the people would become
more contented if the conditions of life were made more
tolerable. This I hold to be the very reverse of truth. As a
workman who has worked from early boyhood on the farm,
down the mine, and in the engineer's shop, I repudiate such a
slanderous statement. What means the continually increasing
restlessness of late years of those workmen who are now,
relatively to their former position, in a passable state of comfort?
I contend that it is in large part due to the additional leisure
obtained under the nine hours system, though most of its
advantages have now been swallowed up by more rapid
machinery and the cursed system of overtime we still tolerate. I
ask myself what has been my guide in the formation of my
opinions on social and political subjects, and, risking being
charged with egotism, I reply that I have ever endeavoured to
get correct views upon these and other subjects by fashioning
my ideas upon the best models I could find, and the more
leisure I had the better my opportunity for finding good
models. I can understand a middle-class man holding this – to
me – absurd theory. I can also understand some workmen
reflecting the opinions of these theory-loving, poverty-
accentuating blockheads merely because they are middle-class.
But I cannot understand a workman who through youth and
early manhood has been battling against long hours in order
that he might attend the institute, listen to the lectures, and
read the works of able men, and by these means has succeeded
in having a mind worth owning – I say I cannot understand
such a one hindering rather than helping in a shorter hours
movement. He practically says by such conduct that the leisure
he used so well as to become a man thereby, others will use so
ill that they will continue fools. But men generally love what is
best for all, and are prepared to do their part towards carrying
it out so soon as they understand clearly what course they
should take. Let those of us who see (or think we see) further
than the average man, do all in our power towards enabling
him to see as clearly as we do, and then, unless I am incapable
of reading aright the lesson of life, he too will become in his
turn an earnest and an energetic worker for the elevation of his
class. I must apologise to some readers who may think that
none of this reasoning is necessary. I emphasise it because I
know there exist philosophers who strain at gnats and swallow
camels, who talk of ameliorating human suffering, but hang
back instead of assisting a movement the success of which must
for a dead certainty largely ameliorate the pangs of the hungry

men, women, and children who are now in the throes of despair.

Another section raise the objection that however desirable it may be to curtail the hours of labour, remembering the severe competition of other countries it is simply impossible either to raise wages or shorten hours unless a similar movement takes place on the continent. I will endeavour to answer this first by showing that the English workers produce more per man than any of the continental nations, and second, by showing that with regard to our staple industries foreign competition is a bogie used by the employer to frighten the workers into accepting harder terms in order that their master may make a greater profit. It may be of some service to point out the relative wealth per annum produced by the useful workers of this and other countries. I am assuming that the reader is clear concerning the source of wealth, that there is no other source than useful labour, so that, having sufficient raw material for workers to exercise their ingenuity upon, it will be seen that the more workers, the more the aggregate wealth, as in all ages men have been able to produce by their labour more than they and their families required for ordinary consumption. Quoting from Mulhall's 'Statistics', we find that Britain with a population of 36 millions produces wealth to the amount of £1,247,000,000 per annum; France with 37½ millions of people produces annually £965,000,000 (or with a million and a half more people about three-quarters the amount the English make), Germany, population 45 millions, wealth per annum, £850,000,000; (or two thirds only of our amount); Russia with 80 millions of people, creates per annum only £760,000,000, Austria, 38 millions population, only £602,000,000 per annum; and similarly with the smaller nations. These figures will serve to show that our method of producing wealth is a more effective one than that in vogue on the continent, as although they generally work longer hours per day than the English yet the result of their year's work compares unfavourably with ours. The important lesson to be learnt here is this, that it is not the amount paid as wages that decides whether or not one country can compete successfully with another; or rather, it is not the countries where wages are low that compete most successfully with this country. This will be seen when it is realised that the severest competitor we have to-day is America, a country that pays at least 25 per cent higher wages than are paid in this country.

This of itself should be sufficient to encourage those timorous mortals who are always attributing our exhausting toil to the competition of the long hours of the continent. The time may arrive when, with an equally advanced method of production, low paid labour will produce wealth as effectively as better paid labour, but that time has not yet come. By way of proving this let me here instance the iron shipbuilding industry. Many have been the disputes between employers and employed in this industry during the past two or three years, the employers continually urging that the continental shipbuilders are getting all the trade, or at any rate will do so, unless our workmen submit to reductions in wages and longer hours. This argument was advanced repeatedly during the year 1885, so in order to thoroughly test the matter a delegation of workers was despatched to the continent to bring back precise information upon the subject. They found that Germany was our chief competitor in iron shipbuilding, and that during the year 1885 that country produced 22,326 tons of shipping. But in this country one firm on the Clyde during the same period turned out 40,000 tons. France produced 10,000 tons, and Russia 7,867 tons – total for the two countries 17,867 tons. But the river Tyne alone launched no less than 102,998 tons. The Belgian output was 5,312 tons, that of Holland 2,651 tons, of Denmark 3,515 tons. To sum up, the whole of the continental output was a little over 50,000 tons, while that of the English shipyards was 540,282 tons, or nearly eleven times as great as that of all the yards on the continent put together. With facts like these before us is it not high time we demanded that our hours were curtailed so as to give a chance to those who now walk about in enforced idleness, without waiting for the continent to take simultaneous action. The Americans, who pay their mechanics better wages, have had to concede the demands of their workmen for the eight hour working day – not universally, it is true, because a universal demand was not made. Just as their success stimulates us, so our success will stimulate the continental workers, and we shall find that they are as well prepared as we are to deal vigorously with the exploiting classes.

To trade unionists I desire to make a special appeal. How long, *how long* will you be content with the present half-hearted policy of your unions? I readily grant that good work has been done in the past by the unions, but, in heaven's name, what good purpose are they serving now? All of them have large numbers out of employment even when their particular trade is busy. None of the important societies have any policy other than that of endeavouring to keep wages from falling. The true unionist policy of *aggression* seems entirely lost sight of; in fact the unionist of to-day should be of all men the last to be hopelessly apathetic, or supporting a policy that plays directly into the hands of the capitalist exploiter. Do not think I am a non-unionist myself, and therefore denounce unionists. I take my share of the work in the trade union to which I belong, but I candidly confess that unless it shows more vigour in the future than it is showing at the present time (June, 1886) I shall be compelled to take the view – against my will – that to continue to spend time over the ordinary squabble-investigating, do-nothing policy will be an unjustifiable waste of one's energies. I am quite sure there are thousands of others in my state of mind – eg all those who concurred with T. R. Threlfall, the president of the Trades Union Congress, when, in his presidential address, he told the delegates assembled at Southport that a critical time had arrived in the history of trades unions, and that in the future they must *lead* or *follow*, and that they could not hope to retain advanced men with their present policy. In his magnificent address Mr Threlfall did all a man could do to stir the unionists up to take action in regard to the eight hour working day, but one looks in vain at each and all of our important trade societies to find any action being taken in the matter. It is not enough to say their funds are low. Their funds are not too low to get up an agitation upon this subject. All over the country they have excellent organisations which might be used in the first place as the means for instructing their own members up to the required standard, and then spreading information amongst the non-unionists, skilled and unskilled alike. When the bulk of these understood the pros and cons of the case the combined forces could make a demand for the immediate passing of an Eight Hours Bill, the details of which could be settled by a duly qualified committee.

While this is being done attention should also be made to another important item alluded to by Mr Threlfall, viz, the payment of election expenses out of the local or imperial rates and the support of Members of Parliament in a similar manner. When this is done we shall be able to command the services of those whom we believe in because of their merits, irrespective of what the depth of their pocket may be.

Let me now invite attention to the effects of an Eight Hour Bill upon some of our monopolies. Let us take the railways as a representative concern, using round figures such as will convey a correct idea to the ordinary reader without confusing him.

The Blue Books bear out the following statements: At the present time the annual income of the British Railways may be put at £70,000,000, of this vast sum one half goes to the shareholders, who do no useful work whatever; one fourth to keep up rolling stock, permanent way etc; and the remaining fourth to the workers (including managers' and superintendents' salaries).

The man who has not paid attention to railway income and expenditure will denounce this as trash or probably by a stronger term. He will probably say that the figures must be wrong, as railway shareholders get only some 5 per cent on their capital. Exactly, but where nearly all make the mistake is in not making the distinction between percentage on money invested and percentage of income. There are nominally more than £920,000,000 invested in railways in the British Isles, and 5 per cent on this means about five-eighths of the total income, the entire income of 70 millions amounting only to 8 per cent on the investments. Consequently a railway company paying $4^1/2$ per cent to shareholders actually pays more than half of the total income to these utterly useless individuals, leaving the remainder to go in about equal proportions to rolling stock and permanent way and as wages and salaries to employees. This gives about 18s per week to the 350,000 persons engaged on railways in the British Isles. When we remember that superintendents and managers get very large salaries, we see that those who do the hard work and have the longest hours get much less than 18s.

Now that we realise the enormous amount the idle shareholders take, let us see how generously they behave to those in their employ. At Nine Elms are situated the cleaning sheds of the South Western Railway. Until recently the 'dirty cleaners' at this yard received £1 0s 6d per week. Instructions have been issued from Waterloo to curtail their wages from 20s 6d to 15s at one stroke. On the same line, at Waterloo terminus, the parcels porters commence work at 5.20 in the morning and keep on till 9.45 in the evening with one Sunday off per fortnight, their wages being from 18s to 22s per week.

Now assuming the average day on railways to be 12 hours, what loss would it inflict on the shareholders if a Bill were passed enforcing an eight hours' working day? We have seen that the employees get about a quarter of the total income or about £17,000,000. To curtail the hours by one third means of course putting one half more men in work than are at present employed. To pay these at a similar rate to those already working would require £8,500,000 or less than one per cent on the nominal value of the shares, so that a company paying 4½ per cent now, would, if one half more men were employed still pay 3½ per cent to the fleecing shareholders. What arrant nonsense then it is to urge that the company cannot afford to curtail hours.

Let us look now at the conditions of our colliers. Here we have men devoting themselves to underground toil from boyhood to old age, the majority never having the opportunity of paying a visit to the capital, or any other large town, practically kennelled in the earth, tied down with capitalistic chains, *'Spending a sunless life in the unwholesome mines'* for the wretched pittance of about 18s per week. Surely an Eight Hours Bill requires no urging from me on behalf of those who work in and about the mines; when we remember that of the value of coal raised annually in this country (about £66,000,000) one third only goes to the colliers who raise it.

An item worth mentioning also was pointed out by Sir Lyon Playfair in his address before the British Association at Aberdeen in 1885, whilst deploring the fact that the exhaustion of the British coalfields made the coal increasingly difficult to get. It was proved that not only has man's ingenuity conquered these obstacles, but owing to the increased power of steam engines and hand-labour-saving appliances, two men now produce as much as three men did twenty years ago. Yet coal is *dearer* now than it was then!

Thirty years ago eight sailors were required for the management of every 100 tons of shipping. Now, owing to improved machinery, less than half that number suffice. In twenty years the consumption of fuel on our ocean-going steamers has been reduced by one half, chiefly owing to the use of compound engines in place of single ones as formerly. Thus on every hand a greater result is being shown with less labour. And it must be so or else there is no meaning in material progress. But 'less labour' means under our existing system, and must mean so as long as industry is controlled by the idle classes, not 'more leisure' or shorter hours all round, but *less wages*, more unemployed, poverty, famine, and physical and moral degradation.

What then can be more rational than to ease the burden of those in work and the starving stomachs of those who are out, by shortening the working day?

See what is going on in the watch-making industry, a fine example of the effects of machinery. Among the exhibits at last year's Inventions Exhibition was that of the Waltham Watch Co. Some machines were there at work making screws for watches, of which it took 250,000 to make up a pound in weight. These machines were so perfectly made, that at the company's factory in Massachusetts, one boy keeps seven of them going. The best wire to make one pound weight of screws costs ten shillings, but after this wire has been converted into screws by passing through this automatic machine, the screws are worth £350, or seven hundred times the cost of the material. Imagine the number of men here thrown out of employment; the watches in large part being made by girls, and the enormous profits going to the owners of the machinery.

Take another case, that of Bryant and May's match factory in East London. Two years ago this firm was formed into a limited liability company. Their work girls are most miserably paid, getting only some 8s per week, and the company refused to increase their pay when they made a demand a short time since. And yet that company, during the first *six* months of its existence, after paying all working expenses, actually paid over £33,000 to shareholders, who had not done a single stroke of work towards producing it. These girls are working ordinary factory hours, 10$\frac{1}{2}$ per day. They cannot live in comfort on such a miserable pittance as they are receiving. How many girls are compelled by this sort of thing, to take to the streets?

The above is only typical of what all our large firms are doing. Armstrong, Mitchell and Co, the great engineering firm at Newcastle-on-Tyne, for instance, last year after deducting for working expenses and depreciation of stock, paid to shareholders £162,000.

Whatever improvement may come through more efficient machinery etc, its effect, while owned by, and used for the profit of, the employing class, will be to throw men out of work and swell the already too full pockets of the capitalists. If we do not decide to curtail the hours of labour, what then can we do? Allow things to go from bad to worse? That is what most assuredly will happen, unless we absorb the unemployed into the ranks of the employed by rigidly suppressing overtime, and curtailing the nominal nine hours per day to something less.

The question will be asked by some, 'What about wages if we work an hour a day less, are we to have an hour's less pay?' Most certainly not. Even when the curtailing principle was only partially applied 15 years ago by the trade unionists this did not happen. On the contrary in many instances the workmen were soon able to get a rise in actual wages in addition to the curtailing of hours. The reason we cannot command a better wage now is because the employer can say, 'If you don't like it you may go, others will be glad to take your place,' but, as I think I have shown, if we make eight hours the labour day when the unemployed will be absorbed and the workers will be able in their turn to dictate terms to the employer.

In conclusion I appeal to the workers of Great Britain to join hands over this business and let us make it a success. In a measure of this kind Liberal and Tory, Christian and freethinker, unionist and non-unionist, mechanic and labourer, radical and social-democrat, teetotaller or vegetarian, whatsoever be your creed or sex, unite on common ground and let us fight this battle of the workers with vigour, with energy and determination. Be no longer apathetic. Take pleasure in the performance of your duty as an honest citizen and the result will be a hastening of that glorious time when the domination of a class shall be a matter of history, and when all shall have enough work and none shall have too much.

CHAPTER TWO

Preachers and Churches*

I make no apology for writing this chapter upon preachers and Churches. In our day every institution is open to criticism, and rightly and necessarily so; and although – if this should meet the eyes of preachers – many of them will doubtless consider it presumption on my part to attempt even to deal with such a subject, let it be so. We live in England, and not in Russia – plutocratic England, it is true, but with democracy getting a good grip. And if by writing this I simply lay myself open to criticism, it may still be the case that I shall have served some small purpose by helping to make clear what it is we object to in orthodox preachers, with their orthodox doctrines and congregations. It cannot be that I am wholly correct, it may be I am very wrong; but feeling strongly upon the subject, and often indulging on Labour platforms in sentiments identical with those I have here given expression to, I now venture (upon invitation) to place before another audience the views I hold, as well as those I condemn.

At the outset, I desire to say that I am fully alive to the fact that there are clergymen, ministers, Sunday-school and Bible-class teachers, who cannot be covered by the general terms of censure I have made use of in what follows. I am happy in possessing the close friendship of not a few who, I am quite sure, are not merely as devoted as any men and women on earth to the cause of truth and righteousness, but strive continuously to make right-doing prevail in every sphere of life. But it is just these who, more than others, feel and know what a terrible responsibility rests upon preachers and teachers as a whole; and who also know, to their sorrow, how shamefully deficient the Churches are in supplying the much-needed correction and stimulus and light.

The Churches set up a claim to be the moral and spiritual guides of humanity, to whom all men should look for guidance as to their conduct in this life, and qualifications for life

* First published in A. Reid (ed.), *Vox Clamantium*, Melbourne (Melville, Mullen & Slade), 1894.

hereafter. The question I propose to examine is: Do they fulfil these functions?

In a complex society like ours, where the average person, on reaching girlhood or boyhood, must perforce begin work of some kind to obtain a maintenance, a very large share of one's time, thought, and energy must of necessity, under present conditions, be devoted to the mere work of obtaining a living. Indeed, it is the paramount question, by the side of which all others fall into comparative insignificance. Consequently, if guidance is needed anywhere, it is in connection with the means whereby a livelihood is to be obtained. The virtues – including honesty, sobriety, and obedience to superiors – are all emphasised in the Sunday schools, Bible-classes, and churches; exactly how to apply them being, of course, too great a task. A general condemnation of 'sin,' and urgent advice to 'flee from the wrath to come,' and find salvation by reliance upon the sacrifice in the crucifixion of Jesus, sums up the teaching of the average school, church, and chapel. Where does this land a man? Judging by a lengthened experience, I unhesitatingly declare that I find that the average church or chapel goer, who is influenced primarily by what he obtains from its functions, becomes a narrow, saving, squeezing creature, taking little or no part in the vigorous life of the community, but very commonly becoming, by his isolated action, a source of weakness in any real democratic movement. If he takes part in municipal or political life, he usually does so on the flimsiest party lines. He generally attributes the cause of the poverty of the poor to their utter degradation, caused by their dissolute habits, brought about by their unchecked evil tendencies, the human heart being desperately wicked and deceitful above all things. Very rarely is he connected with a trade union. As a rule, he is most loyal to the injunction, 'Servants, obey your masters,' and will side with his kindred 'brethren' to blackleg against his fellows.

The tricks of trade he necessarily becomes familiar with; and, like a business man, he not only indulges in them, but becomes an expert thereat. He will attend a prayer-meeting and bless God for the good things of life, and pray for the salvation of the poor sinners in the slums, and will take, as evidences of God's blessing in return, the possession of a few more shares that will pay ten per cent; and if fifteen per cent – why, the more cause for thankfulness, of course! Let none tell me I am concocting a case; such men can be counted by thousands. And why? Because that upon which they have been fed is devoid of real vitalizing force. Instead of giving moral discernment to enable a man to understand how, where, and when moral or, if you will, religious principles should be applied, the preachers land him in a complete fog. Beholding those who are held in high esteem in the Churches, that they include the bankers and stockjobbers, and the company promoters and capitalists and landlords, he follows them rather than the simple carpenter's Son. Between such select and exalted personages and mere labour agitators, trade unionists, socialists, etc., there is, as surely there ought to be, he concludes, a great gulf.

The Church is in a helpless backwash, having lost the true courage, mental and moral vigour, power of discernment, and hence capacity, to apply what humanity now demands. The parsons, clergymen, and ministers are, for the most part, a feeble folk, who, daring not to lead, are therefore bound to follow.

Other men labour, and in the course of years the Church slowly is dragged along; for the pioneers of righteousness we must look elsewhere than to so-called Christians. The man who is truly religious wants no driving to do his duty. He does not try to make all manner of excuses for the exploiters of the industrious community, and pile up the trifling misdeeds of an unfairly handicapped proletariat. A truly religious body of men, whose religion enabled them to understand between right-doing and wrong-doing, and furnished them with the requisite courage to face all foes, would never be content with the sunny complacency of the average parson in the midst of the life-destroying conditions of our industrial centres.

Shame, say I, and a thousand times shame, upon so feeble a religion as that which can tolerate the awful social life which exists in London at this very time. There are not less than four hundred thousand persons in London alone in a state of semi- or actual starvation. There are among these at least a hundred thousand adult males out of work; tens of thousands of women, having no one to rely upon to support them, but in multitudes of instances being responsible for children (or aged or crippled relatives) in addition to themselves, who, over and over again in the course of a year, are deprived of the means of obtaining a livelihood; tens of thousands of children setting off to the Board schools every morning with less than a tenth part of that which is necessary for physical sustenance. Scores of miles of streets, with wretched dens in the background, furnish enormous rents – to whom? To the men of the world? No; to the rich members of your congregations, the great subscribers of your salaries, O preachers! who turn up at your church or chapel service and follow you in praying, 'Thy kingdom come; Thy will be done, as in heaven, so upon the earth.' Can they, do you think, believe that there is anything in heaven corresponding to the wretched slum-dwellers of Whitechapel or Spitalfields? Are there any in heaven corresponding to these Christian rent-takers, who wax fat at the expense of the down-trodden? What are you ministers and plutocratic members of the rich churches and chapels doing to make earth like heaven? Why, it would need an entire change in the basis of society, and the means whereby incomes are obtained. Are these religious plutocrats and preachers trying to change the basis of society, so that better conditions shall prevail? Assuredly not. On the contrary, they are determined opponents of those who do try to make such changes.

The fact is, preachers and congregation are bound hard and fast in a system that is grossly materialistic, utterly soulless in good, and without a single noble aspiration. The Hobbs & Co. Liberator phenomenon indicates how completely swamped is the average Non-conformist soul. Not only did it make haste to get rich, but by the most damnable means that the most cunning Jews and Gentiles combined could devise. Morality! Religion! Where is the religion or the morality in taking ten per cent usury? Yet who among the orthodox in faith and practice objects to ten or more per cent? Honesty! Righteousness! Who that believes in the doctrines of Jesus can uphold industrialism whose very basis from top to toe is ten per cent? 'The man that will not work, neither shall he eat,' is an apostolic injunction; but how many ministers or members of our swell churches and chapels believe it? 'Yes, but even Hobbs and Wright worked,' some will say. Ah, so they did; as did also Mr Charles Pearce of burglar notoriety – the latter with less scoundrelism than the former.

The average preacher or church-goer does distinctly believe, not only that it is right to eat without working, but to get fed, clothed, housed, insured, and buried into the bargain. Who among them condemns as a religious duty the taking of interest and rent? And if these are defended, and I can get sufficient interest or rent to keep me and mine without working, what religious principle comes in after that to say I must work? Or, am I to work like the Yankee millionaire – on six days a week endeavouring to amass the biggest fortune on record, entirely irrespective of how many will be ruined; and on Sunday attending church, receiving the blessing of the minister, and helping to carry the collecting-plate to show how godly I am? If ever Deity was insulted, it is by these devourers of widows' houses, who receive direct sanction and approval from orthodox exponents of orthodox religion. Let none rise to say, 'Oh, but we would never endorse the enormities of the Liberator Company.' If not, where, then, would you stop? The whole shoal of interest-takers and stockbroking gamblers are specimens of the same type in embryo. Not so successful as the millionaire, perhaps – why? Because they lacked opportunity. Never had the brains to scheme like the others, and the courage to come down a resounding crash at the end. Why? Because they hadn't had time to go far enough. The difference isn't in kind; it is only in degree. As in the time of Nahum, so now, to describe London we must indeed say, 'Woe to the bloody city! it is full of lies and robbery.'

I do not state or imply that all this is done hypocritically; what I do say is 'that the truth is not in them.' Christians need to be 'born again.' Orthodox religion is acquiescing in an irreligious condition of Society. Christianity is made part and parcel of the national commercialism, and wholly subservient to the individualistic acquisitiveness of the age. The Fatherhood of God and Brotherhood of Man have come to be mere threadbare phrases when used by an ordinary religionist. Church or chapel is regularly attended, not indeed to obtain guidance out of the industrial and social wilderness, but to maintain tradition and keep up appearances. Some Christians positively believe, doubtless, that religion consists in church-going, hymn-singing, and muttering over the words found in the Prayer-book, or offered up by the minister; failing to realise that these are but the means to an end. If they are used as the end itself, then indeed does moral darkness assert itself.

It does appear to be the case that with industrial England, as with pastoral Israel in the time of Amos, the outward ritual is made the chief concern. At that time the Mosaic ritual was jealously attended to, but the message was:

I hate, I despise your feast-days, and I will not smell in your solemn assemblies. Though ye offer Me burnt offerings, I will not accept them: neither will I regard the peace offerings of your fat beasts. Take thou away from Me the noise of thy songs; for I will not hear the melody of thy viols. But let justice run down as waters, and righteousness as a mighty stream (Amos v. 21–24).

This is a sweeping condemnation of fashionable church-going whilst the state of society is unsound. See v. 11 of the same chapter: 'Forasmuch therefore as your treading is upon the poor, and ye take from him burdens of wheat: ye have built houses,' etc.

Now, it was not the custom even in brutal Israel for one man to literally knock another down in order to take his wheat from him. There were more refined methods of exploitation then as now – though, doubtless, modern civilisation even in Christian England could give the old Jews many points, and beat them at legalised robbery; for it is this legal robbery that is here condemned as much as any other kind.

But nothing puts the case more clearly than the condemnation by Jesus of the orthodox professors of religion of his time (see St. Matt. xxiii. 13, 14) –

But woe unto you, scribes and Pharisees, hypocrites! for ye shut up the kingdom of heaven against men: for ye neither go in yourselves, neither suffer ye them that are entering to go in. Woe unto you, scribes and Pharisees, hypocrites! for ye devour widows' houses, and for a pretence make long prayer: therefore ye shall receive the greater damnation.

No language could be stronger, and yet this was directed against the respectably religious of that day. These Pharisees have their exact counterpart to-day in England.

I know the risk I run by any attempt to deal with the subject of future salvation. But with a keen remembrance of the influence orthodoxy exercised over me – of the years of unrest, of the flimsiness and mimicry with its pretences of solemnity and make-believe solidity – I feel bound to deal with the subject. I know many young men who have striven hard to find 'salvation'; and with blind guides to lead them, many years were spent in finding what ought to have been reached in a few months. The talk about the one thing needful under orthodoxy (it will be noted that I continually guard myself by referring to 'orthodoxy') means nothing more than fixing attention upon Jesus as the Saviour, He having been sacrificed to reconcile mankind to the Father. I make no comment upon this doctrinal point. What I want to expose is the demoralising effect produced by the individual being taught that salvation for him consists in reflecting upon and believing in his acceptance with God, because of Christ's sacrifice, irrespective of the life he leads. 'No one says this,' some will cry. Yes; but, indeed, it is said and taught in nineteen churches out of twenty, and the effect is to cause the individual to think of himself or herself, and to value, out of all proper proportion, his or her own personal salvation. Selfishness begins this, and with selfishness it usually ends. Whilst one can admire the energy put forth and the trouble taken in the voluntary street-corner preachers and singers, one can only pity those who speak, as well as those who may in any way be influenced by what is said. A million times over is the same story told – personal salvation by faith in Christ. It seems to me it would be a truly religious act if all such received a severe castigation for wasting so much time trying to assuage the sorrows primarily brought about by a vicious industrial system, instead of boldly tackling that industrial system itself.

Salvation surely consists in living in accordance with Divine harmony – in loving order and living it – in hating disorder here on earth, and striving might and main to remove it so that earth may be more like heaven. Oh, the unworthiness of followers of Jesus being primarily concerned about their poor little souls! He that seeks to save his soul on these lines will lose it; but he that will lose his own life by working for the salvation of the community – all such must be saved. Up! off your knees, young men! Let us have more effort directed to the removal of evil! Don't go continually begging of God to do that which you ought to do! This world is wrong, and wants righting, and you and I are responsible for doing our share towards righting it. What horrible villainy have you been guilty of, that half your time needs to be taken up in praying for forgiveness? The man that loves righteousness will seek to live righteously, and all such are already saved. His duty is to be at work removing the cause of wrong-doing.

A little less time spent at orthodox mission meetings, and more time spent in helping on effective industrial organisation, to ensure right-doing in the business of life, is sadly needed just now. This orthodox mission work is exactly what our exploiting plutocrats rejoice in. It is so gracious of them to give an occasional ten pounds to keep a mission going, that they may with reasonable safety exploit an additional twenty from their employees, and still receive the praise and blessings of the faithful.

Go to now, ye rich men, weep and howl for your miseries that shall come upon you. Your riches are corrupted and your garments are moth-eaten. Your gold and silver is cankered; and the rust of them shall be a witness against you, and shall eat your flesh as it were fire.

Ye have heaped treasure together for the last days. Behold the hire of the labourers who have reaped down your fields, which is of you kept back by fraud, crieth: and the cries of them which have reaped are entered into the ears of the Lord of sabaoth (St. James v. 1–4).

What have our landed aristocrats and capitalistic plutocrats who go to church and chapel regularly to say to St. James? Dare they claim to be better than those whom James condemned? If so, in what way? And if not, are they not condemned by the book in which they make a pretence of reading? Not that I am affirming that every rich man is necessarily a candidate for hell. What I do contend is that, be we rich or poor, if our mental and moral standard is such that we continue to support the present hellish system – which the ordinary capitalist upholds, and is sanctioned in upholding by the average Church – then we are violating every genuinely religious principle.

I am not condemning religion, but the lack of it. Religion to me consists of those ethical principles that serve as a guide in all matters of conduct – social, political, and industrial alike; and the essence of the whole thing is this: the choice between a life whose actuating motive shall be self, either in acquiring wealth, renown, prestige, or power, and a life which shall have primary regard for the well-being of the community as a whole. To do this is to engage in making it possible for 'His Kingdom to obtain on earth as in heaven.' If I am asked, 'Do I think that all that is necessary is a perfected industrial machinery on socialistic lines?' I say emphatically, 'No! I don't think that is all.'

I do distinctly believe in the necessity for Socialism out and out, and that it is my duty to work for its realisation. But I know also that something more than good machinery is necessary, if really good results are to be obtained. I desire to see every person fired with a holy enthusiasm to put a stop to wrong-doing. Before this is possible, individuals must submit themselves to much and severe discipline. The baser sides of our nature must be beaten down, that the higher and nobler side may develop. Regard for the brethren (brethren meaning all) must be the mainspring of our action; the development of the highest possible qualities in ourselves is undoubtedly a religious duty, but for this chief reason – that we may be of the greater service.

He that would be greatest among you, let him be servant of all.

This to me is the ideal test and standard. As Jesus was the

servant of mankind, so I, as a follower of Jesus, must learn to be of use. The irreligious man is not only the deliberate maker of mischief, but equally so the indolent and useless man. Swedenborg has well said:

All religion has relation to life, and the life of religion is to do good. Further: Heaven consists of those of all nations who love God supremely, and their neighbours as themselves. Hell is the assembly of the selfish – of all who love themselves supremely and gratify their lusts at any cost to others.

The astounding anomaly of our time is the complete separation of religious principles from everyday industrial life. Spiritual pastors teach the young to regard God as the common Father; and when the young become of age to reflect upon the shameful inequalities created and maintained by our social system, they are discouraged by their elders from trying to alter it, and are treated as agitators and destroyers of the peace.

Honesty demands a frank statement that the so-called religions of our time are afraid to apply the principles of Jesus. They make a pretence of championing His cause; but in reality the Socialist agitator and the Trade Union organiser is doing far more than the preachers and the Christians, the Missionary Societies and the Bible Societies to make Christ's gospel prevail. The Churches are afraid of Socialism. Why? Because the wealthy in their congregations are anti-socialists. If any say this is not so, then it will not be difficult to give an effectual reply by quoting instances where the minister has seen the light and dared to proclaim the truth, and where the men who 'have great possessions' (relatively) have very soon taken their departure. I have heard of complaints from one or two such ministers that they not only lost the employer class by their boldness, but that they did not succeed in securing the adhesion of any counteracting proportion among the workers. There is less to be surprised at in this than some seem to think. The Churches having gone astray worse than lost sheep, are not likely very easily to win back democracy. Whether they will ever do it or not is an open question.

The clergyman is undoubtedly at a serious discount as an adviser. 'Serve him right,' say I. Nor will he ever redeem his position except by honest effort on behalf of democracy. Not that democracy will suffer materially if this is not done. The greatest trouble is past. Democracy is learning how to provide for itself, and never was democracy so truly religious as now. And it is gradually getting more so. This religious evolution will increase as the bad environment is altered on one side, and the ethical gospel is lifted up and followed truthfully on the other.

I know that many preachers contend that industrial and economic matters are nothing to them; theirs is a religious work, and men must be left to themselves to find out how to apply religious truths. 'If they were to take sides, it would mean the break up of the Church,' and so on. To endorse a religion apart from principles that are to guide our everyday behaviour is monstrous. If one's religion does not compel one to take sides in favour of a righteous basis of society, the sooner it ceases to encumber the earth the better for all concerned. A minister who can't find time to make up his mind as to the direction in which he should travel on industrial and economic matters, will probably not find time to be of any practical use to the world, nor yet to the denomination to which he may belong. I am fully aware of the fact that by declaring in favour of Socialism, many who might have been disposed to consider the possibility of some mild action favourable to democracy, now stand off. To such let me say: I have purposely avowed myself a Socialist here, so that those who read this may know what I expect from those on whose behalf I can speak. We do not want, and will not have a person's patronage, or goody-goody advice. If there is to be a *rapprochement* it can only be by the parson getting off his high horse, stopping his goodyism and meeting men and women frankly as such. If he doesn't, he'll get left high and dry for a certainty.

I am not here demanding that every parson who is to be of use, shall be an out-and-out Socialist right off. I am telling him that we workmen who happen to be Socialists are adding largely to our numbers every month, that the whole trend of modern effort in our Trade Unions, Co-operative Societies, Town and County Councils, and Parliament is distinctly socialistic, and if parsons and ministers want to stop it, they had better refurbish their weapons. I can easily understand that some genuine men among the clergy will be disquieted by wondering whether the Socialists are coming round their way for a general sharing-out arrangement, and so they are slow to make a move. Such is the enlightenment that exists in these quarters! Let me hasten to reassure all such that if they are to subscribe to the following very mild statement of John Ruskin, they need not be seriously alarmed:

So far am I from invalidating the security of property, that the whole gist of my contention will be found to aim at an extension in its range, and whereas it has long been known and declared that the poor have no right to the property of the rich, I wish it also to be known and declared that the rich have no right to the property of the poor (*Unto this Last*).

That surely should be a self-evident proposition to the mind of a moralist, but it goes rather a long way, as it would mean nothing less than a righteous distribution of wealth. It is to be hoped that no preacher will ask what business is this to him. Surely 'Thou shalt not steal' is emphatic enough, and when we add Carlyle's trifle to it, 'Thou shalt not be stolen from,' it gains a little in clearness. The Church will doubtless concern itself in a few generations to come about such an elementary subject as the enforcement of honesty. We workmen contend that honesty of distribution should become a fact. Forty-nine-fiftieths of present-day poverty, and the bulk of the crime and villainy that now disgrace our country, would disappear, if the Society thieves were to disappear.

But timid Christians and their preachers are likely to reply that, 'to bring about such a change is impossible; human nature won't admit of it.' If not, what becomes of the Lord's Prayer: 'Thy kingdom come . . . as in heaven so upon the earth'? If this is a pious fraud, please be frank enough to say so. Some of us, when we say the Lord's Prayer, do indeed mean it, amongst whom I am glad to be one. I am not willing to be included with those cowards who say it is impossible of realisation. Whatever is right we are bound to work for, even if its fruit is in the dim and distant future. We believe that the Lord's Prayer is not only realisable, but we are of those disciples who will make it so. This done, the question of a 'living wage' will be settled.

As yet in this Christian land we haven't been able to establish a living wage, even when it means nothing more than a sufficiency of material necessities to maintain life. Many in connection with the Churches have recently said that a living wage is impossible, *i.e.* that it is impossible in this 'religious' country to see that each of God's children, our own brothers and sisters, shall be as well fed as a horse. Let Carlyle again be heard

There is not a horse in England, able and willing to work, but has due food and lodging, and goes about sleek-coated, satisfied in heart. And you say, 'It is impossible.' Brothers, I answer, if for you it be impossible, what is to become of you? It is impossible for us to believe it to be impossible. The human brain, looking at these sleek English horses, refuses to believe in such impossibility for Englishmen. Do you depart quickly; clear the ways soon, lest worse befall. We for our share do purpose, with full view of the enormous difficulty, with total disbelief in the impossibility, to endeavour while life is in us, and to die endeavouring, we and our sons, till we attain it, or have all died and ended! (*Past and Present*).

This is the correct spirit in which the modern crusade against our social villainies is to be conducted. It is especially the work of the Church to set the pace. It ought, but we don't expect it will, and yet, I feel sure that those young men and women who are certain to be touched by the devotion and fervour of our modern crusaders, will not require much converting to our side. They are too noble to remain in the ranks of the inactive and selfish. They too will come forth to join in the noble work of social reconstruction. We have a glorious and an inspiriting work in hand – nothing less than the purifying of the industrial and social life of our country and the making of true individuality. For, let it be clearly understood, we labour men are thoroughly in favour of the highest possible development of each individual. We seek no dead level of uniformity and never did. Our ideal is: 'From each according to his capacity, to each according to his needs.' We can't reach that right off, but when we have done so, we shall not be 'far from the kingdom.'

To engage in this work, is to be occupied in the noblest work the earth affords; to do it well, we want not only men and women of good intention – the Churches have these now – we shall want men and women of sound sense who will understand the science of industrial economics, as well as of the highest standard of ethics. To mean well is one thing, to be able to do well is a better thing, and we cannot do well except by accident, unless we know something of the laws that underlie and control the forces with which we shall have to deal. By way of indicating what we hope to reach, it may prevent fear and trembling if I say it is neither more nor less than that set forth by John Stuart Mill, in his 'Autobiography,' where he says:

The Social Problem of the future we considered to be, how to unite the greatest individual liberty of action, with a common ownership in the raw material of the globe, and an equal participation for all in the benefits of combined labour.

Nothing very awful in that surely, and yet there is sufficient to revolutionise modern society! What does a really religious man care how far it goes? To him the one important question is: 'Is it right?' Does duty demand that he shall endorse it and work for its realisation? To me all other duties sink into comparative insignificance. I will yield to none if I know it in facing the straight path, and honestly endeavouring to walk in it. I dare not take my eyes off this big problem.

Much has already been done in removing barriers. The work of the Trade Unionists for the last sixty years has borne good fruit. In the early years of the present century, capital had complete sway. Unrestricted industrial competition was the accepted gospel universally applied in Great Britain. In Parliament the landed aristocracy had complete power. In industrial life, the then infantile but now powerful plutocracy had undisputed control. The law was against combination, consequently there were few Trade Unions. Neither was there anything in the nature of Factory Acts. And what was the result? Our industrial history of that period is the blackest page in England's life. Not only men, but women and children had to work fifteen to sixteen hours a day. Children too, of six, even five years of age, were called to the mills at five o'clock in the morning; if they were a minute late, an overseer with a slave-driver's lash stood there to thrash them and the girls and women like dogs. Some power of revolt existed, and this country owes more than it thinks to the revolutionary course of the early Trade Unionists. We still have England's industrial prestige maintained by child labour at ten and eleven years of age.

In thousands of instances the standard of life is such that when a man is in full work, so little does he earn that the wife and mother must not only get up herself at five o'clock in the morning, but must also wake her children, and take the infant out into the raw wintry air to leave it with some nurse, while she, the mother, must go to the mill, reaching there at six, to take her stand by the men, work all day, and return home at night to commence house duties, and this because the family would starve if she did not. Oh, Church people! if ever a crusade were needed it is here in England now. The honour of our country is left with us to guard. For humanity's sake, let us see to it that we wipe out these accursed blood-red stains. There is much to be proud of in Britain's history, but whilst such conditions remain, we cannot wait to comment upon the work done in face of so much waiting to be done. Who shall do it? Every man and every woman is expected to contribute a share. The social salvation of the entire community is the religious duty in which you preachers and people are called upon to engage.

Oh! rich women of the Churches, have you no social and political duty? You, who spend so much on your own persons, have you no care for the body of society? Yea, I tremble for your future, women of the middle classes, who have a great power; will you not use that power to wipe out these stains on our national and Christian character? If you take up a determined stand in connection with the Churches, they will be compelled to become active. The work will be done with or without you, but quicker with you than without you.

Women! who shall one day bear
Sons to breathe New England air,
If you hear without a blush
Deeds to make the roused blood rush
Like red lava through your veins,
For your sisters now in chains,
Answer! are ye fit to be
Mothers of the brave and free?

CHAPTER THREE

The Socialists' Programme*

A SPEECH DELIVERED AT NORTH ABERDEEN, ON
SATURDAY, 25 APRIL 1896

Friends, – You are probably aware that I am here on the express invitation of a number of electors of North Aberdeen. I am not here to ask anyone to kindly invite me. I would be ashamed of any such behaviour, and hope I ever shall be ashamed of anything that savours of such behaviour. Having accepted the invitation which was duly forwarded, I am glad to know that I am here as the first of the candidates to address an open meeting of the electors of North Aberdeen; to state my principles and my policy fearlessly, fully, and frankly, not caring in the least whether you are pleased with it or whether you are displeased with it.

I have certain definite views which in past years I have advocated as effectively as I have known how. These views will be advocated by me during this campaign, and whether they are liked or lumped, they won't be modified to please the electorate. I shall ask you to remember in the first instance that we are citizens of a country that stands, in many senses, pre-eminent amongst the civilised nations of the world, and I am not insensible to the importance of our country industrially and commercially, neither am I insensible to the voice that our country is capable of exercising the influence she possesses and the commanding position she generally obtains and upholds in the Councils of the nations. Whilst that is so, I wish to make it perfectly clear at the outset, that I am not one who is able to subscribe to the general policy, that because we have what is termed the British Empire, which, in area, is very vast, whose citizens are practically one-sixth of the inhabitants of the globe, and because our country, in particular, is very wealthy indeed, when compared with most civilised nations – I am not prepared on that account to bow down and worship all that is, as though everything were as it ought to be. On the contrary, I come

* First published by Labour Press, Manchester, 1896.

before you as a workman, and in my capacity as a workman, with the responsibilities of a workman's life, having been brought into contact with the rough and tumble side of life, being myself what is termed a skilled artisan, and having been for many years a member of one of the recognised trade unions of our country, which indeed, covers not only our own country, but is international in a genuine sense, covering foreign countries and the colonies; having been also brought into direct contact with the labourer's side of life as distinct from the skilled artisan's, knowing, therefore, what a worker's position is by my own everyday experience, and having carefully studied the general industrial and social situation, I am not, as a result, prepared to worship institutions that exist as if they were even approximately perfect.

On the contrary, I am one of those who have declared my dissatisfaction with things as they are, who holds that the institutions that we have in our country require to be changed in a very important and serious sense, because I know, only too well – and many of you must know also – that there is a very large proportion of our fellow-men and women in the busy cities and towns, aye, and in villages, who are deprived of the means of an ordinary livelihood, not through any fault of their own, but because of an awkward industrial and social environment that they are powerless to control. Therefore are they in the slough of despond, bound down with the bonds of poverty, and as a consequence are suffering most acutely. As an ordinary citizen, an ordinary man of the world, I have recognised it to be my bounden duty during the past, and at this hour, to endeavour to understand what ought to be my individual relationship with other men and other women, not with one section of the community, but with the whole community. I have tried to understand how it comes about that one section of our country can, with very little effort on their part, obtain not only an abundance of that which is necessary for life and well-being, but much more than is sufficient for themselves and those dependent on them, whilst those working very hard and working relatively very long, can scarce get enough of the bare necessaries of life.

In face of the appalling fact known to every student of our industrial and social position, that there are not merely thousands, or tens of thousands, or hundreds of thousands, but actually millions of our fellow citizens who cannot at any time obtain sufficient of the bare necessaries of life – in face of such mental, physical, and moral degradation – I am not prepared to worship the grandeur, the so-called glory of the British Empire. No country can be looked upon as satisfactory that does not afford a proper livelihood for every decently-behaved citizen. Whilst I am not prepared to decry our own country as against other countries, I refuse to be associated with those who seem to find some satisfaction in declaring that a Britisher is a very superior person to any other countryman, and I refuse to subscribe to any such policy because in the aggregate we may truthfully be described as a rich and wealthy nation, that, therefore, all is comparatively well. I know that all is not well, but very far from well, indeed; and therefore, I have been what many persons like to term 'An Agitator,' and I am at this time AN AGITATOR, AND INTEND TO REMAIN ONE.

If the respectabilities of North Aberdeen are not pleased with the general behaviour of such an agitator, there will be no pleading on my part that you should try to. I only want to make a frank, full confession, being, as I have said, utterly indifferent as to what your judgment shall be after you have heard my statement. I do now interchange views with you by asking if you are aware of the standard of life that obtains throughout the length and breadth of our country. When I speak of our country, of course I am referring to the entire British Isles. Are you aware that 24s. per week represents the average wage received by the whole adult male workers of Britain, and that out of that there has to be paid in some districts no less than average of 9s. per week as rent for reasonable accommodation for an ordinary-sized family; and further, that when I describe that as the average – I am using official figures, quoting, indeed, from Robert Giffen, the statistician to the Board of Trade, who, in his evidence recently before the Royal Commission on Labour (of which I happened to be a member) made the statement that £60 a year represented the earning capacity of the ordinary adult male in Britain; now, I venture to declare that £60 per year is not sufficient to secure those means of life and well-being that we may at this time in reason expect to be able to obtain as respectably-behaved and industrious citizens.

PROGRAMME AND POLICY

I therefore ask you to recognise this, that the whole of my programme and the whole of my policy will bear directly upon raising the standard of life for the entire working population of our nation. Holding, as I do, that Parliament should exist primarily for the purpose of contributing to the advancement of those who create the wealth of the nation, in order that there shall be an honest, and therefore equitable, apportionment of the wealth created amongst those who take part in creating it. The poverty, and as a consequence, the crime and misery, that exist are of so appalling a character that we have those who profess to have regard for their removal in almost every rank of life. It is perfectly true that there are such among politicians, that some statesmen can be mentioned, that philanthropists can be named outside the ranks of working men and women, and outside the ranks of those with whom I commonly associate, but whilst that is so, I am bound to ask you to recognise that good intention is not in itself sufficient to remove the serious evils we are burdened with. We must not only be possessed of good intentions, we must have the requisite knowledge to understand the exact why and wherefore of our relatively degraded position, and also must we be able to understand what principle it is necessary to apply in order to rectify the evil. Now, without any disparagement of any individual, or any section of Parliamentarians, I am bound to express my conviction that the average man that seeks to get returned to Parliament is not generally characterised as a student of sociological conditions. The average man, who has sought to get returned to Parliament, and has generally succeeded, has rather been a man of the capitalist or landlord class – classes raised entirely on the shoulders of the real workers – whilst the workers themselves, the actual wealth producers of our nation, have hitherto, for the most part, been content to return to Parliament, and to other places, those very plutocrats and aristocrats who have been living at their expense, and who intend, and have always admitted that they intend to uphold, to maintain, to buttress up the existing orthodox institutions that shall admit in future of a plutocracy and aristocracy living at the expense of a democracy.

DEMOCRACY AND THE SOVEREIGN

I believe I am correct in stating that throughout the world there is now a general awakening to a consciousness that there is something vitally wrong in the constitutions of our various civilised nations: that the caste or class system has hitherto been permitted to dominate over the mass of the people. Some of them are kind enough to declare that the people, unless they are controlled, unless they are guided, unless they are manœuvred, unless they are driven, cannot exist except as so many cattle. Such are the declarations in one form or another made by representative plutocrats and autocrats. And in one country we find a despotic Czar, without any semblance of representative government, who can, at his own sweet will, decree that certain citizens shall be banished for ever from their country, and the order is peremptorily carried out; who can decree that because a man dares to exercise his manhood and express dissatisfaction with the conditions that obtain, that that is to be a sufficient crime to warrant his expulsion from his fatherland, and to carry him to a penal settlement. In another country, we have a despotic Kaiser, who, although there is something in the nature of a representative government, has at present a sufficient backing on the part of the plutocracy that he can and does wield a power and an influence that is distasteful and nauseating to the nature of a really developed man or woman. In another country – our nearest neighbour – we have what purports to be a republican government. It is in a funny position, I am bound to admit, just now, but they are very rarely in other than a funny position. Over this people there is neither Czar nor Kaiser, nor Empress Queen. Nevertheless there is a dominating plutocracy exercising control over the mass of the people, and insisting on a plutocratic domination continuously.

In our own country we have a limited monarchy – a monarch that is respected, and perhaps deservedly so, for various reasons. But all the same I am bound to express my conviction that in proportion as men become men and women become women they will require neither Czar, Kaiser, nor Empress Queen. I am identified with those who hold that an intelligent community should be their own government, if they require a government at all; that to entrust sovereign power, even with various limitations, indicates the relative childhood of a nation, and if it should be the case – as I venture to suggest it is – that the British nation are developing mentally, why, then, the time is approaching when, with much respect – and with much grace, doubtless – we shall be able to dispense with sovereigns altogether. But let none suppose that I place very much value upon that. I have purposely referred to it for the sake of frankly indicating the trend of opinion which I am favouring; but at the same time I know full well that a mere Republican Government, as ordinarily understood, as witnessed in any civilised country that can be named to-day, would do us no good whatever – because none of them have recognised where the real burden comes in.

WHY POVERTY EXISTS

It is for me, therefore, to ask you to please recognise this, that the first essential of civilised life, perhaps also of savage life, are food, clothing, shelter, and some amount of recreation. We have not them in sufficient abundance. Why have we them not? Does not the productive capacity of our people in Britain admit of a much higher standard than that which obtains? The answer is: Yea, for an absolute certainty. If it does, then by what means can we make the requisite changes that shall drive poverty from the land, and establish foundations of peace and plenty? I argue that our prime use for parliament should be to enable the democracy to obtain such control of its own industrial and social destiny, as shall enable them to become triumphant over those conditions.

If it be true, as I allege, that nature has been sufficiently kind as to supply the children of men with all that is essential to real life and well-being; and if it be also true, that our own nation amongst others, has developed the requisite mental capacity to know how to control the raw material of nature, so that with a wise expenditure of power we possess, with comparative ease, we can produce enough and to spare for everybody, why, then, it becomes our bounden duty to endeavour to understand how it has come about that we have not as yet applied that power wisely, and why we should still require workhouses, jails, street-corner loafers, beggars by the hundred thousand, and ne'er-do-wells in increasing shoals. You require the ne'er-do-wells on the one side, with the jail birds and the slum dwellers, because on the other side you tolerate the system, acquiesce in the system, and have approved of the system that encourages and upholds and maintains, and affords scope and opportunities for company promoters and all that pertains thereto, who live by fleecing, by scheming, by dodging, by trickery, by rascality, and by developing all the qualities that enable them to prosper. And it has generally been that the more successful the exploiter, the greater readiness has been exhibited on the part of the electorate to return such a one (because he has been successful, forsooth!) to the Legislative Assembly in order that there he can continue to exercise a dominant influence, socially, industrially, and politically. But apparently the eyes of a portion of the electorate are being opened, and now there is less satisfaction in fighting for a man simply because he occupies an important position in the social scale; there is less satisfaction now in returning anyone unless they have previously been subjected, as it were, to a cross-examination, and their desires understood and their principles examined and approved of. I do not for one moment pretend that the electorate of Great Britain is remarkably wise; but I think we are warranted in saying that we are getting a little wiser than we were; and if anyone should be disposed to apply this and say, 'Well, we shall show our wisdom by rejecting you,' I shall still acquiesce with the greatest grace and thankfulness. All the same, I ask you now, is it not the case that you and I as citizens of this country, responsible like other citizens for families, being desirous of discharging our duties in a becoming and honourable fashion, unwilling to live at other people's expense, but not being specially desirous that other able-bodied people should live at our expense – is it not admissible or desirable that we should seek now to apply very definite principles for the rectification of these defects? Are there any here whose social condition is such, or may have been such, that they have never hungered for a meal, who have never known, except by hearsay, what it is to be in want, and who sometimes wonder whether there are any unemployed apart from those who are really indifferent to work? If there are, then I ask you to please put yourself to the trouble to understand the facts of the case, and if you are willing to go, even to the governmental sources – which are not always distinctly favourable to those who are unemployed – and you will find even from such a report as that issued monthly, 'The Labour Gazette,' through the agency of the Labour Department of the Board of Trade, that the proportion of unemployed, as registered by the various unions, is positively appalling compared with what you have probably thought has been the case. I need not trouble to dwell upon this, but I will quote Carlyle: 'Do you notice the horses in the street, and see how relatively well-fed and sleek-coated they are, and are you disposed to urge that it is impossible for British citizens to be equally well fed with British horses?' Such was Carlyle's question, such is mine; and I declare to you, and you know it to be true, that there are hundreds of thousands of British men, women and children whose actual condition is much inferior to the ordinary cart-horse. Carlyle said: 'Do you ask whether it is impossible to obtain as good conditions for British men and women? If so, then clear out of the way and make room for better men and women.' I reiterate Carlyle's statement, and declare that those with whom I am associated – and I hope they will not consider it egotistical – have vowed as men and women may be permitted to vow, and, like Carlyle declare, that for ourselves and our children who are following us, we will spend ourselves in the endeavour to secure to the men, women, and children of our country, at least as good conditions as we now give to the ordinary cart-horse.

THE WAY TO PEACE AND PLENTY

The cautious will be disposed to say: 'Of course we can endorse so elementary a statement, but we are not all sure where you would lead if you had the chance.' Then I will tell you by quoting one simple sentence from the autobiography of John Stuart Mill, who ought to be known, and, I presume, is pretty well-known in this district. Speaking, I believe, for himself and his wife, he said: 'The social problem of the future we consider to be how to secure the greatest individual liberty of action, with the common ownership of the raw material of the globe, and the equal participation by all in the benefits of combined labour.' That is the basis upon which I am here to-night. That is the economic basis upon which I am running this election campaign; and if any of you – press included – desire to argue against my Collectivist principles, do not forget that, at the same time, you must argue down the Collectivist principles, clearly expressed, of John Stuart Mill. If you will say that John Stuart Mill was not identified with our particular school of thought, I am prepared to admit the fact, seeing that John Stuart Mill died some years before it was possible for him to be closely identified with it. But if anyone is prepared to fairly face the question, and try to understand the attitude taken up by Mill in his early years, his middle life, and towards the close of his life, then I think that you will be disposed to declare, that in quoting this sentence, I am quoting Mill's state of mind when he wrote that autobiography, and when doubtless he was in the fullest possession of a developed intellect. And what he saw was forthcoming has come. The social problem he spoke of as being likely to arise in the future, we are living right in the front of; we are in that particular stage when we must face the social problem. I am therefore proposing to deal with the methods whereby we will attack this social problem and try to solve it. The desire is to place within the reach of every properly behaved citizen all that is essential to real life and well-being, therefore we must not have excessive work, and we ought to have enough work.

THE EIGHT HOURS QUESTION!

To-day the unemployed do not get enough, and the overworked, of course, get too much, and that lands us right off into the very simple statement and contention, that surely it is desirable that there should be an adjustment with regard to the working hours of men and women of our country. The very just and simplest statement that can be made is that, as we find there are men working no less than 16 hours out of 24, and that other men who would be equally capable of work, and who would be glad to have the opportunity of working, are without work, and are suffering in consequence, surely good sense says let us ease up on the one side, and give a little work to the other side. Therefore, it is that the various Trade Unions of our country, as well as other labour sections, have for years been discussing the desirability until they have now reached the position that they say it is absolutely necessary that there should be regulation of working hours, and they have declared in favour of an eight hours working day as being one of the simplest and most practicable steps that can be taken to rectify some of the industrial and social evils of our time. If anybody should be disposed to say that this cannot cure the unemployed problem, I can accompany you in that, but I say it could do a good deal towards rectifying the evils we are now deploring. And it is right and proper and becoming from an economic, industrial, and from a social standpoint, that we should so regulate the working hours. In the first instance, surely it is desirable that not more than eight hours should be spent in obtaining a sufficiency of the bread that perisheth, if we can produce enough in that time. Surely, it is desirable in the interests of men and women who are already actually at work, and even more desirable is it for those men and women who have not the chance to work at all, and who should be afforded an opportunity by those who are working excessively! I know, of course, that it has been said – and probably with a considerable amount of truth – that in certain departments of industry men can soon learn to produce as much in eight hours as they were formerly producing in nine and ten, and good luck to them for being able to do so. But there are many departments of industry where that would be impossible for a very considerable time, and all that there is to be said is that, as soon as we reach a period when as much work can be done in eight hours as can be done in nine or ten, then let us come down to seven, or even six. And if it should appear rather stupid to any of you, then I ask, how do you propose to distribute the advantages of our nation's material progress? If it be true that year by year we are gaining a little over nature, and are capable of producing in five hours, and at a little later stage in four hours, that we formerly produced in six; how would you distribute, but by easing the daily burden all round, and generally equalising the reward of labour? Surely, of all measures, the one that ought to commend itself to the average man and the average woman is that for the regulation of working hours. I am, therefore, in favour of an eight hours' working day for the whole of the trades and industries of our nation. And if any should be disposed to ask: 'Would I refuse to accept any measure that was not really national,' I say 'No, I would not refuse.' If for instance, as happens to be the case, the miners made a special effort, as they have done, to demand an eight hours' day, and having, as I consider they have, very special claims for attention in this direction without waiting for the general volume of the nation. If I were in the House I should continue, as I have done out of it, to advocate the reasonableness, wisdom, and the good sense on the part of the miners in insisting on the application of eight hours as the maximum working day in their industry, and if a little later other industries should be disposed to make advances, out of proportion to the general body, I should, of course, be prepared to back up their demands, and to do all in my power to see that it was applied to them at the earliest possible moment; but I declare fearlessly and frankly in favour of a maximum eight hours' working day for all.

TREATMENT FOR PHYSICAL WRECKS

That would do something towards solving the unemployed problems, but it could not really solve it. I know that something else would be necessary, and I know there are many classed as unemployed who are at the present hour physically unfit for labour for various reasons. They have been out of work too long a time, they have had insufficient food, and live in unhealthy conditions generally, and they cannot compete in accordance with the demands of the competitive system, nor are they likely ever to be able to, unless some special steps are taken, I therefore declare in favour of the State, that is the executive of the State, in conjunction with the various local governing bodies, taking such action as shall afford a reasonable outlet for the energy possessed by persons like unto whom I am referring. By this I mean that just as I, the father of a family, am bound to have regard for every child for which I am responsible, whether the child be capable or not, as compared with some others, is not the child's concern, it is my concern, and so with regard to the State. If we believe in Constitutional Government, if we believe in the community's Executive, if we are disposed to use it in the interest of the democracy, why, then, who will say it is not the duty of such an Executive to have regard for those who have been the victims of an awkward environment? Surely that is quite fair as a matter of common humanity. I ask that it should be recognised that those who have been victimised, from whatever cause, should have special attention paid to them, and I believe it would become quite an easy matter for the Executive Government along with the local administrative bodies, to obtain control of the land in the right districts, and place those persons either upon it, or in industrial undertakings in connection with such a colony, and thus make it possible for them first to receive the requisite training, and then to become actual producers of what they require to consume, and probably, at no distant date, of a margin over and above that. And if there are any disposed to say, 'Ah, but it would be a tax upon the community,' remember that, from the fact that they are living, they are a tax upon the community now. There is no jailbird or street-corner loafer not living at the community's expense, and what I am proposing is simply a scientific method of providing for their requirements, and doing it in a becoming and dignified way that shall not disgrace our common humanity.

PRODUCTION IN GREAT BRITAIN

In conjunction with this, I would ask you to recognise that the British nation is not producing a large proportion of food-stuffs it consumes, and it is held by many, and by many whose opinions I think are worth noting, that it is desirable, aye, and becoming very necessary, that we should produce in Britain a larger proportion of food-stuffs than we now do. The fact is we produce only one-third of the food-stuffs we require to consume. It is not because the land will not yield, it is not because the requisite good sense does not exist, but it is because there has been a general rush to produce wealth by the capitalistic section in the easiest possible fashion, irrespective of the well-being of the community.

Without trying to put the blame on any particular shoulder, I simply ask that it be recognised that the day is rapidly approaching when British commercial supremacy will be seriously questioned and threatened. Nay, not approaching; it has approached, it is right here – I would remind you that the Right Hon. John Morley quite recently referred to the fact – I think on the occasion of his last speech at Newcastle-on-Tyne, that every year brought us intensified competition from every Continental country, and that now we were to be confronted with the competition of Eastern nations. That means, of course, that Japan and China and India are all entering to cater for the world's markets, and therefore British supremacy, industrially speaking, is very seriously questioned. What the orthodox man has propounded is that the British worker shall buckle to, and by one means or another overcome the foreigner, and beat him and drive him to destruction. I tell you I despise and hate such a doctrine. Tell me that the only way for my salvation is, as it were, to drive somebody else to starvation and desperation, and I refuse to have salvation on those terms. I for one do not regret that the Continental nations are learning to produce commodities which were formerly produced by Britain, but, of course, that carries with it the absolute necessity of understanding in what direction we can develop our energy, so as to balance the requisite production of food-stuffs with the production of manufactured commodities. Therefore, I anticipate that Britain must learn to produce more food-stuffs than she has done, because other countries will produce more manufactured commodities than they have done. And there is no earthly reason worth consideration why they should not do so, as, of course, there is no real, sound reason why we should not be more a food-producer and perhaps a little less a producer of coal and iron and other hardware. I ask you, therefore, if you endorse the ordinary commercial principle that what you have endorsed as part of this principle is increased and intensified competition with every European nation, with America, and now with the Japs and the Chinamen. If you can look forward to that, I cannot, and I do not want the support of those who can. I tell you plainly that I would be ashamed to subscribe to a policy that tells me I can only get food for myself and family, and other men like me, by fighting down and driving to despair other men equally courageous, equally lovable, and equally unobjectionable in every way. I therefore call for such attention being given to agriculture as shall enable us scientifically to divert the surplus energy from industrial pursuits to food-producing channels. This will bear rigid investigation, it will bear the investigation of scientific experts, and it will bear the investigation and receive the approval of the sound economists of the country.

CHILD LABOUR AND PENSIONS FOR ALL

Now, a friend on my left shouted, 'The women first.' I admire his gallantry. I ask that it should be recognised, that all who are in a relatively helpless position should receive prime attention, therefore, I call for scientific attention being given to children. Their labour does not obtain in Aberdeen to the extent that it does in some other towns in Britain, but I believe it does obtain to a far greater extent than we would look upon with approval. Now, I know that the income of the ordinary parents is not sufficient to enable them to live in comfort, unless they get all that is possible through the agency indicated. But remember, I have subscribed, and do now subscribe, and ask you to try and do the same, to that definite kind of organisation that lands you into the Trades Union movement, to fight for and obtain – as men responsible for your families – a sufficient income to enable you to behave with requisite dignity, so that you can maintain your home without having to resort to the labour of mere infants. Therefore, I am opposed to infants going to work at twelve years of age even, and I should be glad to see, and should work for a raising of the age, at the earliest possible moment, to something considerably higher than that I have indicated, before children should be called upon to labour in the mills, the factories, or the workshops. Another important question that I am bound to work for, and that I think would commend itself to you, is adequate provision in the form of pensions for all industrial soldiers, for all genuine citizens who have laboured and have reached that period of life when assistance is absolutely required, because they are not in a fit condition to provide for themselves under the old conditions. Then they ought, as a matter of right, having worked in their day and contributed to the community's well-being, to receive from the community what is requisite for their adequate maintenance. Therefore, I am in favour of pensions for all, irrespective of the positions they occupy, and always making, of course, for that position when there shall be equality of opportunity for all, and when we shall approximate to equal conditions. Remember, I include here the infirm and the sick as well as the elderly. Every infirm person, every sick person, irrespective of the causes, should be cared for by the community, in the interests of the community, as well as in the interest of the child.

NATIONALISATION

With a view of bringing about that state of genuine cooperation I look forward to, instead of this capitalistic system, we call for the nationalisation of the railways and waterways of our country. It is a sin and a shame that the railways should be primarily controlled in the interests of shareholders rather than in the interests of the industry of the country and of the travelling public. Ere long I shall expect to see developed that volume of opinion that will call for the control of the railways and waterways of our country by the community's executive in the interests of all, affording every reasonable facility for the opening up of the country to agriculture and to industry generally. I call for the nationalisation of the mines and minerals of the country. The minerals are the gift of nature, and are not by moral right the property of any one handful of the community. I am identified with those who would at the earliest possible moment undertake to control them and regulate their output through the agency of state regulation, and not leave it to the caprice of the individuals who to-day control them for their own selfish interests. We must declare that the surface land must be common property. Land was not made by man or woman. It is the gift of Nature to the common children of men, and it is not for you nor for me nor for anybody above us or below us to exercise a monopoly-power over it. That we should have tolerated it so far is not very complimentary either to our intelligence or to our courage. I know the day is some distance off when land nationalisation is likely to be successfully carried through the British House of Commons. I, therefore, expect to see changes made in the direction of common or collective ownership, by adding to the power of the local governing bodies. We have further South, Parish Councils, of a somewhat different character from yours. It is an administrative body, exercising functions other than those of the Parochial Board; but you, as well as we, have County Councils and District Councils, and we call, and I am now calling for the requisite power being invested in these bodies, so that through the agency of the State they may be enabled to obtain from the present owners, such land as the residents in the respective districts may be willing to cultivate collectively, paying rent (for rent will always have to be paid) to the recognised communal authority, and therefore securing to community all the advantages of the unearned increment which hitherto has gone to the mere landlord, who has done nothing whatever to produce it. In the seven points I have now enumerated, I have given

SEVEN DEFINITE PRACTICAL PROPOSALS

If you should be disposed to say, 'Oh, but the country is not equal to it yet.' Why, what is Parliament for, and what are we for, and what are you for? To wait until somebody else can lead, and then you are to follow? I am not going to do that. I tell you in the plainest language that I will refuse to be a drag weight upon political opinion, and I refuse to be an observant of Mrs. Grundy, that I will not dare to speak the faith I have learned and understand, and I will not subscribe, if I know it, to any spasmodic or erratic policy; and I hope to be able ever to retain sufficient mental vigour and love of genuine progress as to dare to step out of the ordinary orthodox rut and to say: 'This is the way: Walk ye in it.' If you cannot, I will, anyway, or perish in the attempt. If you are disposed to say: 'Where is the money to come from to enable these changes to be made?' then I must remind you of certain facts – that the workers who produce the wealth of the nation do not receive more than one-half of that which they produce; that about one-fourth of the total community, as Chamberlain once said, and he himself is included – toil not, neither do they spin, yet are they arrayed in much magnificence at the expense of those who do. I ask you to recognise that, through the agency of a graduated income tax, we would gladly rectify the anomalies that to-day exist, and provide adequately for all the changes I have suggested. If any of you are disposed to say: 'Is it idealism, after all?' I am not prepared to go back on my idealism, and I will not give one inch to any man amongst you for definite, practical, detailed, solid work, calculated to build up a newer and better country than we have yet known. I ask you to understand that if you and I know each other more closely, I will refuse to be a nonentity. I will refuse to be kicked and cajoled, but I will always be willing and glad to be consulted and to consult you. I will try to understand exactly your particular requirements, as the North Division of Aberdeen, but I will never pretend that Aberdeen is heaven and everywhere else is hell. I am, and intend to remain, cosmopolitan, but it does not debar me, or in any way prevent me, from giving every reasonable attention to local requirements.

I am prepared for any kind of opposition. Fearing no one's power, courting no one's favour, I state my case as a workman, who, if returned, would have some satisfaction in trying to fight on the floor of the House of Commons as I have endeavoured to fight outside, for those principles of truth and justice and equity, as I understand them, hoping thereby to contribute to the day when poverty shall be banished and peace and plenty shall prevail, when swords shall be beaten into ploughshares, and spears into pruning hooks, when nation shall not lift itself up against nation, shall learn war no more, and when brotherhood and sisterhood shall really be an established fact, with all the blessings that follow in its train.

CHAPTER FOUR

Socialism*

Socialism has occupied the attention of certain sections in Europe for fully a generation, and during the past twenty years those using the English tongue have gradually been forced by circumstances to recognise that Socialism imperatively demands attention at the hands of all and sundry who can by any fair means be classed as Social Reformers, or even as intelligent Politicians.

At the present time, 1905, the politically and socially active citizens in every civilised State and Nation, find it increasingly necessary to have some knowledge of Socialism and Socialists.

In writing this brochure my object is to contribute a little towards a correct knowledge of an admittedly vast and important subject.

Those who are disposed to try and understand the numerous questions involved in such a study, should first try and realise that this science of Sociology should be approached as impartially and as deliberately as the exact sciences say of Astronomy or Geology: The student should try and divest himself of preconceived ideas, which he has imbibed from his surroundings, and not as the result of study.

Knowledge will certainly prove helpful in the long run, and it is worth while taking trouble to understand correctly the arguments for and against the subject to be dealt with. Above all, it is desirable that the man who wishes to be correct should take the pains to understand what is to be said against the subject he may have a predilection for, and therefore if this falls into the hands of any who have not studied the subject and such should become favourably impressed by reading the same I strongly advise them to study what the opposition has to say. A sensible man is not anxious that any particular 'ism' shall prevail, he is only anxious that the *Right* conditions shall obtain.

* First published by 'Tocsin' Office, Melbourne, 1905.

HOW TO JUDGE OF WHAT IS RIGHT,

will be dealt with later on.

A searching investigation into fundamental basic principles is at all times to be encouraged. If Socialism disappears in consequence of such investigation, it will be because it ought to disappear and make room for something that will bear the searchlight of scientific analysis.

It will give a stimulus to study if one reflects upon the astounding development of the study of Sociology during recent years. Not only is it true that in every country are to be found educated persons systematically dealing with the subject but the science is rapidly taking front place in many educational establishments. The professors at the universities are amongst the most ardent disciples of this science of human life, involving as it does a knowledge of ethics, politics, and economics. Not one State or Nation can be named which has not a definitely organised body for the furtherance of the objects of Social Democracy, this latter term being quite as freely used as Socialism, but considered by many to be more specific and definite. It is the term used by the Germans, who found it necessary to distinguish between the State Socialism of Bismarck and the Democratic Socialism of the People.

The Social Problem which it is the object of Social Reformers to solve, is many sided, and may be expressed in a variety of ways. But there is no difficulty in grasping the main essentials: Briefly put, it may be said that to study the Social Problem is to study the causes of poverty and the effects of poverty, but if there is no desire to get rid of poverty with a view to establishing conditions of general well-being, there can be no recognition of a Social Problem. Immediately one reflects upon the subject, one is confronted with this remarkable fact, that the power of the people of to-day to produce wealth is many times greater than at any previous period in the known history of the World: at the same time, poverty is so prevalent and terribly acute, that every week that passes, many

THOUSANDS OF PERSONS DIE

because of insufficient nourishment. Another notable fact is, that those who suffer so acutely are not merely those who are careless, indifferent or idle, but equally those who are and have ever been most careful, sober and industrious. Further, it is found that Republican and Monarchical Countries suffer alike, that Free Trade and Protectionist Countries have exactly the same characteristics. That whether a Tory Government or a Liberal Government has a comparatively long innings in any given country, the results are just the same to the vast majority, to probably ninety per cent of the population, and no real difference of conditions obtains re the workers' standard of life, though it may, and sometimes does (especially in America) result in a re-shuffling amongst civil servants, changing the particular persons that will fill certain official positions, but in no way changing for the better the conditions of the toiling masses.

The enquirer soon notices the tall talk indulged in by certain sections in practically every nation, as to the exceptionally good conditions that prevail in that Nation; as a literal fact there is no State or Nation existing under conditions that will secure the means of a bare livelihood to all its people, no matter how willing and able they may be to work if they get the opportunity.

The student will discover, that in countries with a relatively sparse population like Australia, it is held that what is needed is more people, in a relatively densely populated country like Britain, it is said the cure will be found in emigration, or by getting rid of the people. In France, where density of population is much lighter than that of Britain and much heavier than that of Australia, but where the proportion in want is just about the same as in both countries named, they are told it is the competition of Italy that keeps wages low, yet France is a Protectionist Nation. In Germany and Belgium they are told it is the competition of England that necessitates such arduous toil for so little in return, and yet the difference in the standard of life, such as it is, is higher in England than the other countries named.

In the United Kingdom again the workers are frequently told that they spend

AN UNWARRANTABLE AMOUNT ON ALCOHOLIC LIQUORS.

Thus in the Non-Socialist ranks, there is the utmost confusion as to the causes producing poverty, and equally great confusion as to proposed remedies.

Consider then a few of these facts: We all know there is poverty in every country, and all well intentioned men are deeply sorry for this. It is known that Food, Clothes, Shelter, and all other commodities are the direct product of labour, spent upon the raw material provided by Nature. It is also known that there is an abundance of raw material to adequately supply the wants of the whole world without any concern, and it is further known, that the power of men to produce the requirements of life from this raw material is very much greater than ever before, and yet in every country people die of starvation. It is also known that the raw material, *i.e.* the Land and Minerals, are constantly available. It is further known that the people require to be fed and clothed and otherwise provided for constantly, and it is still further known that Land Minerals and Machinery are lying idle, and hundreds of thousands of men are in enforced idleness, such incongruities would be unbelievable if we were not in daily contact with the facts. Is there a solution to these intricacies? Let no man conclude there is not till he understands what there is to be said. Let no man conclude he is here asked to discard all other proposals and give attention only to Socialist proposals. On the contrary, let each do his best to refrain from endorsing Socialism, but resolve that he will examine every proposal worthy of attention, and give to each what is due, but if he finds it necessary he will endorse and work for Socialism or any other 'ism' that satisfies his reason is equal to the requirements of the case. Not the backing up of an 'ism' or 'ology' but

THE ABOLITION OF POVERTY

and securing good conditions for all without exception, should be our guiding principle.

It may be said it is very well to tell us to endorse those principles and policies that will effect a solution of the Poverty Problem, but how is one to decide when there are so many advisers? All that can be said in reply to this is, a man must trust his thinking faculties, trust no-one's proposals without investigation, and honestly endeavour to gauge the nature of the proposal advanced. It may be taken for granted that those who are not willing to know the best and strongest that can be brought against a system are lacking in training or honesty.

How can a man tell when he is a Socialist? It may be asked: is there a clear line of demarcation between the Socialist and Non-Socialist? and the reply is, beyond doubt it is a very easy matter to understand the essentials of Socialism, the endorsement of which means that such a person is a Socialist and the non-endorsement of which forbids the term Socialist being applied.

It is not an uncommon thing to find persons expressing sympathy with Socialism and Socialists, when all that is intended by them is, a kindly feeling towards those in poverty, but by no means do they endorse the Co-operative Ownership and control of the Land, Mines, Minerals, Machinery and Agencies of Transit, without which no-one can be a Socialist.

By Co-operative ownership is meant ownership by the whole people, i.e. the Raw Material and Machinery of Production to become the property of the public, and industry to be regulated by experts in the common interest, and the reward for work done to be according to the amount performed; otherwise put, under National Co-operation or Socialism, or Social Democracy, or Collectivism (all of which mean the same), working hours would be regulated according to the amount of work to be done, and the number of people to do it, the workers engaged in the less pleasant kinds of work would probably work fewer hours than those in the more agreeable occupations.

Once again then,

SOCIAL DEMOCRACY, OR SOCIALISM

involves the transference from present day private ownership to National Ownership of all those agencies of wealth production, necessary for the supply of life's necessaries for the whole people. The root basis of this is found in the fact that private ownership of the means of wealth production fails most lamentably to provide all the people with the commodities of life. Let that fact never be forgotten, private enterprise utterly fails at the present time to conduct trading operations in such fashion as to admit of honest and earnest-minded men and women obtaining for themselves a sufficiency of the necessaries of life, and in addition there are children by the million who are never surrounded with healthful conditions. Let no man dare to begin quibbling about the particular methods of the transference, all morality, all true religion, unsophisticated humanity, cries aloud for such changes as may be necessary to afford the means of healthy vigorous life for All.

But whilst many may see the force of this, they may not see why it should be really necessary to change from private ownership to public ownership of the means of production.

To make this clear one must get a correct idea of the incentive to action on the part of the capitalist section of the community; and the first item of importance in this regard, is to realise fully that the object aimed at by the Capitalists who own the land and other raw materials, and by the Capitalists who own the Machinery and Ships and Railway appliances, and by the investing owners of capital, is purely to obtain profit, therefore the present system is properly termed a Capitalistic Competitive System aiming at making further profit by each Capitalist section, but never aiming at securing the public welfare.

This is not saying that Capitalists are badly disposed towards the Community; they may be, as undoubtedly many of them are, perfectly honest and well disposed towards all *according to Capitalistic Morality, i.e.* according to what is considered moral behaviour under the present civilised regime. Nor could they be part of the present system and behave much other than as at present. But watch the effects! Capitalists own and control industrial establishments in every manufacturing country, and the means of obtaining trade is by competing in the world's market against all other Capitalists in the same trade also seeking a share in the market; to compete effectively, they must place the commodity on the market as cheaply as or cheaper than other competitors. In order to do this they must ever have regard to cheapening the cost of production, and the bed-rock policy pursued in purchasing raw material to be worked up into the finished commodity, and also in the purchase of labour force, is to purchase as cheaply as possible and sell as dearly as possible. Therefore they keep wages down to the lowest possible margin; there is not an exception to this rule, it does not follow that an employer will necessarily be ever trying to reduce the wages of the men, there are two conditions generally operating to make that difficult, the one is the organised power of the workers to resist encroachments of the kind, and the other is that generally speaking men who receive the highest wages are really the cheapest producers, but what the Capitalist ever aims at is the paying as wages of the lowest proportion possible of the total product of the Factory. In short, as Karl Marx long ago explained, the Capitalist is always after the 'surplus value,' *i.e.* that the largest possible amount of the total value produced in the establishment shall come to him as profits, and therefore that the least possible should be absorbed as wages, expenses of management and general up-keep of the establishment.

It necessarily follows that each group of Capitalists is continually on the look-out to save wages, and therefore every new device in the way of what is termed

LABOUR SAVING WHICH IS REALLY WAGES SAVING
MACHINERY

is made use of, and the result is that there is a constantly
diminishing proportion of the total produce of labour going in
the form of wages to those who perform the labour, and a
constantly increasing proportion of the total out-put going as
profits to the Capitalist. Not a trade can be named but confirms
this contention. That is not the worst phase of the matter. It
will be seen that with the ever increased power to produce
commodities the market is stocked with increasing ease, and by
men who have been engaged in producing serviceable
commodities producing so very much more than they receive in
wages and therefore more than they consume, the markets are
glutted, and these same men are thrown into the ranks of the
unemployed, not because they have failed to work effectively,
but because they have produced so abundantly and consumed
so little of it, they are therefore discharged and prevented from
getting even a sufficiency upon which to live. This is the direct
effect of private ownership of the means of production for the
purpose of making profit for the Capitalists, instead of working
Co-operatively in the common or public interest.

Let the anti-Socialist think over the above statement and
meet it if he can. We Socialists declare that the whole world
bears witness to the truth of the statement as to the effects of
production for profit for Capitalists, and that being so we
declare the present system stands condemned.

It will be seen that the very same means whereby
manufacturing and commercial success is achieved, are also the
same means that carry degradation to the workers, and there is
no possible escape from this so long as private enterprise
dominates the industrial system by which all must live.

Thus the argument so frequently used by the opponents of
Socialism, that private ownership and control are the only
means whereby a stimulus can be obtained, or an incentive to
action provided, has no possible chance of operating excepting
upon a trifling minority of the population. On the present basis
the sooner the markets are glutted the sooner will the workers
be unemployed. The more the workers contribute towards
facilitating production the smaller will be the proportion of
their total number in employment: where then does the
stimulus come in to encourage the highest possible?

A MORE GROSSLY UNFAIR SYSTEM THAN THE PRESENT COULD NOT BE DEVISED

It is commonly said by opponents that under Socialism we should all become Slaves of the State. It is well to ask what amount of freedom the worker enjoys to-day. A small percentage of wage receivers are doubtless in receipt of a relatively high wage, these are quite necessary to the Capitalists to ensure the successful whipping up of their fellows, and are found in the most highly developed form in the United States of America, they number about eight per cent, of the wage receivers; quite ninety per cent are ever under the direct regimentation of the Capitalists, or are enjoying the freedom of being out of work, including the freedom to walk about begging for work and failing to get it, and the further freedom of walking back home to enjoy the comforting sight of a starving wife and children. Yes indeed we are living under free conditions to-day, the freedom can be witnessed in most countries in the marches of the starving unemployed. In America there are one and a half millions of men unemployed, 'ten millions of our citizens are in abject poverty and forty millions more of us are in fear of poverty.' See *Wilshires Magazine*, May 1905, East 23rd St, New York.

In England, unemployed marches, Demonstrations and Conferences have at last resulted in a Bill being introduced in the House of Commons by the Government purporting to deal with the subject. The 'Daily News' (London) just to hand, gives a graphic description of bootmakers on the march from Northamptonshire to London 'led by a cripple on crutches, behind whom walks the band, with a half dozen much worn and battered instruments,' the number of *bona fide* unemployed in the UK at the present time is estimated by Mr Keir Hardie MP at seven hundred and fifty thousand, and this is supported by trade union statistics.

In Sydney a few days ago a procession of the unemployed was marching toward Parliament House when the Police interfered, and broke up the procession. In the Melbourne 'Herald' of June 14th, is the following statement. 'There is, we regret to say,

GREAT DISTRESS AMONGST THE FAMILIES OF WORKLESS MEN

in this city, a sum of £10 was sent to us for distribution. It is sad to have to report that the claimants for participation are so numerous that in no case has it been thought desirable to give more than five shillings, and the greater part of the money is going in mere bread-and-butter doles of half-a-crown per family. The would-be bread winners protest that it is work they want not charity.' I personally can vouch for the truth of these statements as I have attended many of the meetings of the unemployed, I know a number of them personally, and accompanied a deputation of them to the Hon. John Murray, Minister of Lands. Such being the conditions, it would be a waste of time to further dwell upon the inadequacies of the present system to make even tolerable provision for all citizens, and those who take up the position of opponents to Socialism lest we should all become 'Slaves of the State,' would do well to realise that economic enslavement is now the lot of a large portion of the workers of all countries.

Some opponents find satisfaction in declaring that Socialism has been tried many times in various countries and has 'always proved a failure.'

By this is generally meant that in various places at different times, small groups of persons, betimes considerable numbers, being dissatisfied with the conditions under which they lived and worked, and having some desire to work on a Co-operative or Communist basis, have banded together and tried the experiment. None of these attempts has been of a genuine Socialist character, although many of them have been Socialist or Communist in tendency. The scientific Socialist accepts and advocates principles which he believes must inevitably prevail consequent upon the development of modern Capitalism, which having out-grown its usefulness is rapidly preparing the ground for Socialism; but it has never been possible for Socialism to prevail in any modern State, seeing that the State itself as an organised entity is essentially bourgeois or plutocratic. Every Government that can be named has been brought into existence for the express purpose of maintaining

THE DOMINATION OF THE PROPERTIED CLASS,

and to keep under subjection the proletariat or property-less class. So long as individuals belonging to the property-owning and dominating section, continue to exercise control and ownership of the means of production, and decide as hitherto they have ever decided the character of the Law and the control of the judiciary, no country is ready for Socialism. Socialism can only exist when the people collectively own the instruments and agencies of production and distribution untrammelled by sectional monopolistic power, wielded by a selfish Plutocracy.

It is not in the power of any group or society to lift itself out of the pernicious influence of sectional monopoly, whilst it is in the midst of a world where every Governmental department, Naval, Military, and Civil alike, is manned exclusively in the interest of Plutocracy. Why then should people attempt to form Societies of the kind, it may be asked? Chiefly because good men and true get tired of waiting for the full evolutionary development of Capitalism, and its natural supercession by Socialism; and being able to see and compelled to feel the terrible faults of a Plutocratic Capitalism and yearning to get to a better state quickly, they seek to take short cuts thereto and frequently get squashed in their precocious attempts.

This applies to those who try to lift themselves out of the maelstrom of Capitalist influence when every department and institution controlling all that is best in the world is under the blasting influence and ownership of the Capitalist Class. When Capitalist Politicians or the Capitalist press scoffingly urge the advisability of Socialists commencing operations on a Socialist basis in a Capitalist State, it is about as much to the point as though the Co-operative owners of a few tugboats wishful for freedom to roam the North Seas as they pleased were told by the British Admiralty they were at liberty to do so, with the knowledge that in the British Fleet the Admiralty could at any hour not only hem them in but sink them immediately they desired, by their monopolistic control of the only effective fighting forces.

Some seek to attach importance to the attempt made to establish what was termed

'NEW AUSTRALIA,' IN PARAGUAY ON A COMMUNIST BASIS.

As is well known the prime mover in this was William Lane, and a splendid fellow he was, exceptionally well informed, very capable within his own limits, whole-souled and honest hearted, he tired terribly of the Maritime Strike of 1890, and the Shearers' great struggle in Queensland in the following year. Further, William Lane had as comrades some dozen men of much more than average ability and devotion, all of whom appear to have joined systematically in the discussion of the New Australian project, but scarcely one of whom shared in Lane's sanguine belief as to the wisdom of the project: Lane being strong of will, appealed to whomsoever would to join the expedition, and of those who left Australia for South America, not five per cent were communists or Socialists, some of them had no knowledge of the main principles or belief in any ideal other than 'getting on,' the result was forseen, and predicted by Lane's best Socialist friends who have been and are still battling away in the movement in Queensland.

Even so, much success was met with, and the promise was bright, allowing for the inevitable disadvantages all such projects must be subjected to, till owing to difference of opinion perfectly natural and to be expected, one portion decided to leave the 'New Australian' Settlement and to establish another, with little to work with, at Cosme; and still much success attended the efforts of the Cosmeites, until William Lane himself decided to abandon the attempt apparently disheartened at the lack of Socialist knowledge and spirit manifested, and even then it continued, though with varying success, and William Lane's brother Ernest has now returned to Queensland, pretty good evidence that there is not much to be expected from Cosme.

On the other hand several attempts of a similar character in the United States have proved permanently successful, and the religious body known as the Shakers, has been able for generations past to completely abolish poverty and to organise industry in an absolutely successful fashion for themselves.

As to the attempts at anything in the nature of

CO-OPERATIVE OR COMMUNIST COLONIES OR SETTLEMENTS, UNDER THE AUSPICES OF CAPITALISTIC GOVERNMENTS,

nearly all such attempts have been made as part of a panic-stricken policy when the pressure of the unemployed has been unusually severe; and not infrequently those in authority have deliberately aimed at discrediting any attempt at a Socialist experiment. Thus in France in 1848, after Louis Blanc had repeatedly urged the establishment of National Workshops and the organisation of the unemployed, when the crisis was reached the Ministry in power declared they would act upon the suggestions of Louis Blanc and try to guard against further difficulties, and immediately when they gave the authorisation for the National Workshops, they appointed as General Director, Emile Thomas, a chemist who had been, and still remained, a bitter opponent of Blanc's principles and proposals. Blanc immediately protested and declared nothing but failure would result, and such was the case deliberately arranged for by the authorities. So with the South Australian settlements, when men with only the usual ideas of commercialism are placed under conditions calling for the exhibition of qualities they have never understood or at any rate never thoroughly appreciated, in the nature of things, failure must result.

Therefore it is that Socialists generally discourage isolated socialist settlements, surrounded by Capitalist influences and Monopolies, and always subject to the machinations of the astute Plutocracy. But this by no means condemns the principle of the State organisation of the unemployed, on the contrary, now that some amount of democratic influence is being exerted in the respective Legislatures, a manifestation of its usefulness should be looked for in this direction.

Another of the fallacies that pervades the ordinary mind not versed in industrial and social matters is, that what is wanted above all things is an addition to trade. The Free Trader and Protectionist alike advocate their respective views on the plea that if their views are acted upon, an addition to the volume of trade will be the result and therefore all will be well,

WORK FOR UNEMPLOYED, HIGH WAGES, SHORT HOURS AND GENERAL PROSPERITY.

And yet every country claiming to be civilised is continually adding to its volume of trade: As this phase of the subject appears difficult for many to grasp, it becomes necessary to deal with it at sufficient length. By way of enabling this to be understood I will take the case of the United Kingdom, where it is known that many suffer from unemployment, from low wages, from inadequate housing &c., and then come the proposals for increasing trade, to get rid of these hardships, and yet the trade of that country has been constantly increasing for the past three generations. In fixing upon the United Kingdom for the purposes of illustration I do so because most Australians are more familiar with and interested in that country than in either of the others, and also because the Australian press, and politicians and many workmen habitually refer to the poverty that exists there and proceed to argue that something should be done to check the decline of British Trade. It should then help in learning a useful lesson when it is known that there is no decline in the total volume of trade nor yet in any of the staple industries, but a very considerable increase. There has been in recent years a greater aggregate output and greater output per capita.

Thus a London Magazine, 'The Social Democrat,' for January, 1905. 'So far as statistics of imports and exports are evidence of national well-being, ours is steadily on the increase. The value of goods imported during last month was £52,800,000 as compared with £52,300,000 in the corresponding month of the previous year, and £48,200,000 in December, 1902. For the twelve months ending last December, the imports amounted to £551,400,000 as compared with £542,600,000 in the previous year, and £528,400,000 in 1902. The exports again show for December of last year £34,500,000 as against £30,400,000 in December of the previous year, and £29,600,000 in December 1902. The total exports for the last twelve months amounted to £371,100,000 as compared with £360,400,000 in the previous year, and £349,200,000 in 1902.' These are the figures issued officially by the British Board of Trade.

Who has not discussed

BRITISH ENGINEERING AND SHIPBUILDING DURING RECENT YEARS,

and who has not shared in the view that British Trade was seriously declining and hence the unemployed?

Therefore it will be interesting to learn the facts. The Board of Trade figures show that the total exports of machinery and millwork having been £21,082,502 for 1904 as compared with £20,058,206 for 1903, and £18,754,815 for 1902. Commenting on this says Mr. Geo. N. Barnes, General Secretary of the Amalgamated Society of Engineers in his Annual Report, 'These figures form a strange and strong commentary on the lamentations which have been made about alleged loss of foreign trade, and they have also as strange and strong a bearing in connection with the question of the unemployed, the number of whom have been increasing concurrently with this increase of orders from abroad.'

'There was a decrease in the tonnage launched from 2,536,731 tons in the year 1903, to 2,422,941 last year. Of the total tonnage launched 1,332,337 tons were from British yards, and 1,090,604 from yards other than British, the decreased output from British having been 10,171 tons, and from other yards 103,619 tons, from which it appears that British builders more than held their own during the year.'

Those who have been commenting so strongly upon the serious inroads made into British Trade will probably find it a little difficult to reconcile matters; it is worth while in this regard to remember that Britain's total population is 42,000,000 out of a world's population of 1,700,000,000 and yet Britain builds and engines many more vessels than the rest of the whole world besides.

Ah! yes, say many, but it is in electrical engineering where Britain is losing ground. Is it? Judge by the following—

At the last meeting of the British Association, Professor Walthier Lotz read a paper before the Economic Section. This was published in the *Manchester Guardian* in which 'a statement of the position of 59

GERMAN ENGINEERING FIRMS FOR THE YEAR 1904

is given, and it is found that not a single one of them made a profit, but on the contrary some of them show immense losses, amounting in some cases, to over £50,000 sterling, and many of them had paid no dividend for two and three years.' For the British position the engineering supplement of *The Times* (London) Newspaper, supplies the necessary information which is reprinted in the April number, 1905, of the Amalgamated Engineers Journal. Sir Chas. McLaren, head of the Palmer Shipbuilding and Iron Company, John Brown and Company, and other industrial enterprises, says that; 'In machinery, engine building, and first-class railway material, competition has', he says, "done us little harm" and, as a rule, work has gone to other countries from British and Indian railways only when our own shops have been full; and he further says that "high profits are in many cases made from year to year, salaries are paid to managers and officials far above anything which can be earned by way of fixed emoluments in any other profession'"; '*Re* Electrical Engineering' another *Times* Supplement writer says, 'that the total capital for the United Kingdom "in this industry" was £61,109,525 in 1896, and at the end of 1904, £266,926,270, an increase of over 400 per cent.'

The object aimed at in giving these figures, all of which are from absolutely reliable sources, is not to indulge in the nonsense of claiming superiority for the British, but to show the utter unsoundness of the arguments of those who would account for the degradation of a large portion of British workers by wrongfully declaring it is 'due to a falling off of trade.'

In order to complete the argument it will be well to give the results of the labour of the people of that same country as estimated not by Socialists only, but by the recognised Statisticians of the Plutocracy. Thus,

ON THE AUTHORITY OF SIR ROBERT GIFFEN

fifteen years ago the National annual production of wealth in the United Kingdom equalled £1,250,000,000 (twelve hundred and fifty millions of pounds), and nearly one half of this or £600,000,000 (six hundred millions of pounds) went to those who produced it all, brain and manual workers included, salaried persons, wage receivers and that portion classed as profits which was really the wages of superintendence, leaving more than one half of the total or £650,000,000 (six hundred and fifty millions) to go to the receivers of Rent, Interest, and Profit, for which no service was rendered to the community, therefore the producers received less than one half of the value produced, and the Capitalist Plutocracy really exploited the actual producers of more than one pound out of every two pounds of value produced. At that time the population of the UK numbered 36 millions, in 1904 the population had increased to 42 millions and the wealth produced equalled £1,750,000,000 (seventeen hundred and fifty millions) an increase of no less than £500,000,000 (five hundred millions) but only a very small portion of this extra amount found its way to the mental and manual workers who produced it all. Their share was £750,000,000 (seven hundred and fifty millions) whilst the non-working exploiting Plutocracy, received £1,000,000 (one thousand millions) for doing nothing. These are the nuts for the Anti-Socialists to crack. What is the good of talking about the poverty of the British or Irish people being due to bad trade in face of such facts as these? With such facts before us how puny is the talk of the fiscal adjusters when they declaim about the poverty of the old country!

To leave no loophole of escape for opponents, and to further buttress up the position, it will be helpful to give the actual wealth per head of the various countries of the world; not the value of the annual product, but the existing accumulated wealth. This is made an easy matter, as Mr. W. McLean the Government Statist of Victoria has himself compiled the statistics, or given the authorities on which he bases his statements, and has issued the same in the 'Victorian Year Book,' issued 1905 in an article entitled 'Accumulation.'

Private wealth of Principal Countries of the world per inhabitant:

	£		£
United Kingdom	302	Germany	156
New South Wales	266	Belgium	154
Victoria	261	Argentine	154
South Australia	260	Europe	139
France	252	Spain	135
New Zealand	246	Sweden & Norway	114
United States	234	Australia	104
Denmark	230	Greece	101
Canada	196	Danubian States	90
Holland	183	Portugal	87
Switzerland	164	Russia	61

Can it be plainer shown that the root cause of poverty in the UK is not lack of production but faulty distribution? and it is exactly the same cause in Australia; When this is rooted and grounded in one's mind, no worker or well-wisher of the people will go frantic about a change in fiscal policy, hoping thereby to add a trifle to the total volume of trade, as though that ever yet gave any security of well-being to the workers. A high production is of course desirable, and will certainly be resorted to under Socialism, but no matter by what percentage the volume of trade increases under a Capitalist regime, poverty can never be extirpated thereby.

Opponents of Socialism often declare that there are so many definitions of it that it is well nigh impossible to know exactly what Socialists are after. To do a little towards removing this ground of complaint I will give definitions of a sufficiently general and precise character that no readers of this pamphlet shall be able to say they cannot tell what Socialism is. First, briefly what it is not. Socialism does not seek to destroy individuality, but to make it possible for each person to develop his or her faculties up to the highest possible pitch of perfection.

Socialism does not seek to destroy but to build up, to build fine cities, in which shall be the most magnificent edifices the mind of man can conceive, where every building whether for public or private use shall be architecturally beautiful.

SOCIALISM DOES NOT AIM AT MAKING ANY THE
SLAVES OF GOVERNMENTS,

but to gradually and surely get rid of all Governments other than the self-Government of free and intelligent citizens.

Socialism does not aim at robbing the rich but at preventing the rich from continuing to rob the poor.

Socialism does not favour or tolerate promiscuity between the sexes, but sternly declares in favour of Monogamy.

Socialism does not enjoin upon its adherents the acceptance of Atheistic principles, but leaves all perfectly free to enjoy whatsoever religious belief commends itself to them.

In defining Socialism it is necessary to guard against that which is Socialistic in tendency, and Socialism of a full fledged character. Socialism is the recognition and adoption of the principle and practice of Association as against isolation, of Co-operation as against Competition, of concerted action in the interests of all, instead of 'each for himself and the devil take the hindmost.' Socialism saddles upon each of us the responsibility of being our 'brother's keeper.' If a child, woman or man is starving, Socialism says there is something wrong in our social system, and upon us all individually and collectively rests the responsibility of righting the wrong. If one street or a dozen streets contains one slum dwelling or a number of such, Socialism says to each of us jointly and severally, 'crime exists somewhere or no slum would exist, see to it quickly, root it out, raze the slum to the ground and let air and sunshine operate.' If men are overworked and so prevented from fully sharing in the joys of life, Socialism bids us to immediately remove the causes of overwork and see to it that every man and every woman shall have a fair share of all that makes life worth living.

All this is true, but it is not true that Socialism can be summed up as a mere tendency. There can be no real Socialism where exploitation obtains, under Socialism no person can live idly upon the labour of others by receiving unearned income in the forms of interest, profit or rent. Therefore

SOCIALISM MEANS THE COMPLETE SUPERCESSION OF
THE PRESENT CAPITALIST SYSTEM,

of private ownership and control of Land, Machinery, and Money, necessary for reproductive purposes.

Therefore those who do not believe in the necessity for and the justice of the Nationalisation of the means of production should not call themselves Socialists. It is not fair to the Socialist movement, and sooner or later it will land the person who vaguely covers himself by an unwarrantable term in a serious difficulty.

Above all I would ask that no one shall consider it necessary to patronise Socialists or Socialism, whilst not believing in the principles. We Socialists are well used to buffeting our way in the World, and much prefer to stand or fall by our bed rock principles. With us there is no whittling down or begging of any one to accept our assurance that we are 'not as black as we are painted.' Word painting at our expense, or for our decoration, perturbs us very little, the fight has been fought now for many years and it will be carried on by us with increasing vigour; and to be 'tolerated' is against our grain, believe and work with us, or fight us, that is our attitude.

To understand the Socialist position one must have some root grasp of morals. For our purpose at the moment it will suffice to say, that right conduct or morality means, proper relations between ourselves and others, *i.e.* behaviour of a helpful and useful character. Under no set of circumstances must one take an advantage of one's fellows; fair play between each and all, universal honesty, and right conduct not for one day a week but for every day of every week, is essential. Therefore to forcibly take from another that which is his, is a violation of right conduct, and equally so, if by making use of circumstances that places another in our power we may politely consent to take advantage of him, it is also a violation of right conduct. The reason being that it deprives another man of his rightful opportunities to develop along equally good lines with the rest of his fellows, so, when one section of men exercises a monopoly power over the agencies whereby other men must obtain the means of life, and

THE MONOPOLISTS REFUSE ACCESS TO THESE AGENCIES

by those who must get them or die, and the Monopolists stipulate for, or in any case exact that, the users of these agencies shall pay to them one half of the value produced, by those who will engage in wealth production, this is as gross a violation of morals as anything known in human history, and when in addition to this, those who would use these agencies find it impossible to produce (under the vicious conditions brought about by the Monopolists) a sufficiency to maintain themselves and satisfy the Monopolists, that the Monopolists then refuse the would-be users of the wealth producing agencies the opportunity to use them, even though it means starvation and death, it gives point to the grossness of modern notions of religious behaviour and orthodox morality, which not only tolerate but approve of such monopoly.

We therefore declare that the present Capitalist system is based upon the legalised robbery of the wealth producers by the Land Monopolists, Machinery Monopolists and Financial Monopolists, and the undoubted object of Socialism is to get rid of these Monopolists as speedily as possible.

All Socialists of every country agree with the statement made. There are differences of opinion as to the particular kind of action, political and economic, that shall receive immediate attention, and there are some who would not use Parliamentary action at all for the realisation of the object, but none would disagree with that object as stated.

Exactly when we may expect to see this object realised, and what particular month or year we shall celebrate the realisation of a Socialist State it would be rather premature to speculate upon, and some who claim to be Socialists declare 'that the transition to Socialism will be so gradual as to be imperceptible, and that there will never come a day when we shall be able to say,

NOW WE HAVE A SOCIALIST STATE

To such cautious souls I reply that although there is much truth in their contention that the process will be gradual, we shall be able to say that we have a Socialist State on the day on which no man or group of men holds, over the means of production, property rights by which the labour of the producers can be subjected to exploitation. Hubert Bland in Fabian Essays, p. 214, 1889.

But how, if Socialist aims are not in accord with true politico-economic development? Why then those aims will never be realised. None know and admit that so clearly as Socialists themselves. In the early days of Socialist advocacy the orthodox political economists pretended to flout as unscientific the contentions of the Socialists; they declared that nature had stipulated we must for ever fight each other on the basis of 'the struggle for existence – the remorseless extirpation of the weak – the survival of the fittest – in short, natural selection at work. Socialism seemed too good to be true: it was passed by as merely the old optimism foolishly running its head against the stone wall of modern science. But Socialism now challenges individualism, scepticism, pessimism, worship of nature personified as a devil, on their own ground of science. The science of the production and distribution of wealth is Political Economy. Socialism appeals to that science, and turning on Individualism its own guns, routs it in incurable disaster. Henceforth the bitter cynic who still finds the world an eternal and unimprovable doghole, with the placid person of means who repeats the familiar misquotation, 'the poor ye shall have always with you,' lose their usurped place among the cultured, and pass over to the ranks of the ignorant, the shallow and the superstitious.' George Bernard Shaw, in Fabian Essays, p. 28.

Students of political economy are encouraged to keep to their studies, the only danger lies in a lack of study. John Stuart Mill is often quoted by the Individualists as a bulwark of strength, they conveniently forget that Mill became a convert to Socialism and in his Autobiography declares that, 'The Social Problem of the future we considered to be, how to unite the greatest individual liberty of action, with a common ownership in the raw material of the globe, and an equal participation for all in the benefits of combined labour.'

There the whole

SOCIALIST POSITION IS FULLY CONCEDED AND AVOWED,

and the individualists' champion takes his place on the side of the Collectivists.

If it is asked, 'Do Socialists intend to deprive the present monopolists of their Monopolies without compensation?' The reply is that that entirely depends upon the Monopolists themselves. If they are wise and recognise the forces rapidly gathering strength and reasonably facilitate the necessary changes on peaceful lines, the community will without doubt allow and accord generous compensation, but if on the other hand they behave rebelliously, and refuse to come to reasonable terms, the community will stand none of their fooling, and they will be placed under restraint until they come to their senses, and recognise the wisdom of participating in the changed order.

It suits the present purpose of the rich and their backers to express terror at the prospect of being despoiled of their property, the object aimed at by them is to divert attention from the actual robbery systematically conducted by them. 'This robbing the poor because he is poor is especially the mercantile form of theft, consisting in taking advantage of a man's necessities, in order to obtain his labour or property at a reduced price. The ordinary highwayman's opposite form of robbing – of the rich, because he is rich – does not appear to occur so often to the old merchants mind; probably because, being less profitable and more dangerous than the robbery of the poor, it is rarely practised by persons of discretion.' John Ruskin, in 'Unto this Last,' and again in the same volume says Ruskin, 'So that, the art of becoming "rich" in the common sense, is not absolutely nor finally the art of accumulating much money for ourselves, but also of contriving that our neighbours shall have less. In accurate terms, it is the art of establishing the maximum inequality in our own favour.' Chap.: On 'The Views of Wealth,' p. 46.

And still again says the grand old Teacher, John Ruskin, in the same volume, 'So far am I from invalidating the security of property, that the whole gist of my contention will be found to aim at an extension in its range, and whereas it has long been known and declared that the poor have no right to the property of the rich, I wish it also to be known and declared that the rich have no right to the property of the poor.'

The same lesson is emphasised by Thomas Carlyle when he urges the workers to always remember the injunction,

'THOU SHALT NOT STEAL,'

but never to forget its corollary, 'Thou shalt not be stolen from.'

Socialism stands for the Abolition of Robbery and the Abolition of Poverty. The opponents of Socialism seek to defend the effete individualism now rapidly tottering to its fall, it has served its purpose and nature herself is rapidly clearing it out of the road.

Could evidence be plainer of the strong trend of modern development from private ownership of productive agencies, than is to be found in the remarkable growth of municipal enterprise to be seen in every country in Europe and America, and beginning to show itself in Australia? The means of transit, Railways, Trams, Buses, Cabs, Ferry Boats, were in the hands of private Monopolists; during the last fifteen years the bulk of these have become the common property of the people with enormous advantage to the entire body of citizens. So, with regard to water, Gas, and Electric Light and Power supply, these were privately owned and controlled, but private ownership proved a ghastly failure in comparison to collective ownership by the people as a whole, managed through and by the democratically elected public authorities.

All the principal cities of the World either already have or are now engaged in establishing industries that were formerly entrusted to private enterprise; Public ownership and public administration have proved to be immeasurably superior to private ownership on private profit making lines. The Capitalists of the world know this, and fear the effects to themselves as privileged Monopolists, when the Government Machinery of the States is used to transfer the larger industries under the ownership and control of the common people. In municipalisation is to be seen

THE ACTUAL APPLICATION OF THE SOCIALIST PRINCIPLE,

although it is wholly impossible for more than a little of the advantages to come to the people as yet, whilst all the Financial Institutions are owned and controlled by private Monopolists. As it necessitates that the people shall borrow back at a high rate of interest a portion of the capital they have themselves created, in order to apply the principle of Public ownership. Further, the reactionary Politicians in every Parliament, variously named as Tories, Liberals, Republicans, Democrats and Fiscal Reformers, have done their utmost to check municipal enterprise, but the natural evolutionary forces have swept them aside and the achievements of the people's duly-appointed experts have accomplished results wholly impossible to private profit hunters.

Take the writings on Municipalisation of Dr. Shaw of America, take the achievements of the French, the Germans, the British, through and by Municipal ownership, and the advantages are so tangible, so real and thorough, that great as the drawback is of private Monopoly in Finance, not one State or Nation thinks of going back to private enterprise, but in every case without a single exception, the order is to extend public ownership, and get rid of the incompetence of private monopoly. Already we have passed the stage of experiment, the principle is definitely established, and those who are vainly endeavouring to checkmate the growth of Socialism, would save themselves from humiliating ridicule if they dropped their futile attempts at 'bogey' raising. Whilst they are declaring that all attempts at Socialism have failed, all civilised countries which have sampled collective ownership and control for the public good, and contrasted the results with private ownership and control for private profit making, are in ever increasing numbers demanding further extensions thereof.

Much public attention has been occupied by the critics of the Australian Labor Parties, more particularly because New South Wales, Victoria, and Queensland, have definitely declared in favour of the Nationalisation of the means of Production, Distribution, and Exchange, as the ultimate object of the respective Parties. This one fact warrants us in declaring that Australia is perfectly safe for Socialism. During the past two years particularly,

THE CAPITALIST PRESS HAS BEEN EXCEPTIONALLY BITTER

in each of the States named, and every kind of Capitalist organisation has been resorted to, to vilify the Socialist Movement and its advocates. The Plutocrats have now the reply of the workers and know how successful their efforts to thwart Socialist propaganda have been.

At the elections in South Australia a month ago, the fight was declared by the Capitalist faction to be Socialism or no Socialism, the reply was given by the electors, who instead of returning only six straight-out pledged Labor Candidates as in the previous Parliament, returned no less than fifteen out of a Legislative Assembly of 42.

The comrades throughout the whole of Australasia extend their fraternal greetings and hearty congratulations to the comrades of SA and particularly to those who fought so excellent a fight, not less to those that were not returned, than to those who were, and specially do we extend greetings and good wishes to the Parliamentary Labor Leader, Mr. Tom Price, whose duties will soon be of a heavy character, to him and to his Parliamentary Colleagues all good wishes for successful battlings in and out of Parliament. The South Australian Labor successes are most encouraging and augur well what we may hope for and realise in the immediate future.

In Queensland, exactly one half of the Legislative Assembly has been returned on the straight Labor ticket, i.e. 36 in an Assembly of 72. Mr. Geo. Kerr, MLA for Barcoo is the Parliamentary Leader of the Labor Party, and all admit him to be an absolutely honest and earnest man; but Mr. Kerr belongs to the canny old Northumberland stock, so many of whom are pronounced individualists in politics. Consequently Mr. Kerr as President of the Labor-in-Politics-Convention held in Queensland two months ago, not only did not favour the inclusion of

SOCIALISM, AS THE DECLARED OBJECTIVE OF THE PARTY

but felt it his duty to oppose it. Mr. Kerr was within his right in so doing, as were also his four State Parliamentary Colleagues who voted with Mr. Kerr in the minority of ten: viz: Messrs Burrows, Jackson, McDonnell and Turner. The voting on the Socialist Objective was, Ayes 28, Noes 10, a pretty clear indication of the direction the rank and file are taking.

It was very interesting to me to listen to an able and eloquent speech from Mr. Geo. Kerr, MLA, on the desirablity of the Federal Labor Party, accepting the same objective as agreed upon in Queensland, delivered in Fitzgerald's Circus Buildings, Melbourne, on July 9th, on the occasion of a reception to the delegates to the Inter-State Conference, of whom Mr. Kerr was one.

It was encouraging to find such a clear pronouncement given, as since the Coalition Government a general flatness had characterised the Queensland Labor Party in and out of the House. Although having half the membership of the Lower Chamber returned on the straight out ticket, the Labor Party have been content with only two of their number occupying Cabinet positions, Messrs. Kidston, as Treasurer, and Peter Airey as Home Secretary. The present Government is known as the Morgan–Labor Coalition Government. Differences of opinion exist as to whether it was wise for the Labor Party to enter into such an alliance or Coalition, but it was acquiesced in as the speediest way of getting the State Franchise broadened on to the basis of adult suffrage, instead of the old narrow multiple vote system that formerly obtained. This Franchise Act will become operative at the next State Election and the Labor Socialist successes will be commensurate therewith.

That there is urgent need for effective work on the part of the Labor Party every one will admit who knows the industrial and social conditions that obtain. In the Sugar growing trade 95 per cent of the white population work eleven hour shifts. All the Sugar Mills and Refineries run 24 hours with only two shifts of men, and the wage averages about 25s. a week and 'tucker'. This work lasts for about six months in each year when all but the mechanics are discharged, to 'Hump the Bluey' for the next six months, averaging not more than one week's work a month for the period. At the meat works there is nothing in the nature of an eight hour day, nine, ten or more prevailing. The Butchers of Brisbane work seventy-two hours a week as against forty-eight for Slaughtermen and fifty for Shopmen in Victoria, where organisation has received more attention. The Banana Trade, a very extensive and profitable business, is exclusively in the hands of the Chinamen, not only for growing, but for dealing and marketing also. There is indeed plenty of work to engage the attention of the Political Labor Party, but if it is to be accomplished, industrial organisation must receive attention also. The Sea-going engineers are about the only ones effectively organised as far as my experience goes. Certainly the Engineers ashore are not; as a member of the

AMALGAMATED SOCIETY OF ENGINEERS

I carefully enquired how matters were, and learned as regards the Government Railway Shops at Ipswich, that employ 640 persons all told, 160 of whom are eligible for membership of the ASE, only eleven were members of that body, nor do they belong to any other industrial organisation; I was not surprised therefore to learn that the wages of these skilled mechanics are nine shillings and three half-pence per shift. The Miners of Gympie, Charters Towers, Mt. Morgan, Mt. Perry, and Chillagoe all stand in need of organisation. In every other State and Nation wherever political action on advanced lines is in the ascendant, industrial organisation is also on the increase.

It was my privilege to meet many excellent fellows at nearly every town I visited between Brisbane and Cairns, and the better they were the more they admitted the urgent need of organisation; so much so that I feel safe in predicting there will soon be a considerable change for the better in Queensland, and trade organisation and political action will travel together.

In New South Wales, Labor men have been particularly active during the past four years in the matter of industrial organisation. Five years ago there were not more than ten thousand trade unionists in the whole State, now there are 70,000, this is the result of the State Arbitration and Conciliation Act, the workers have organised so as to register under and receive the benefits of the Act, which in the vast majority of instances have been substantial in the matter of reduced working hours, and increased rates of pay. The workers' representative has at all times proved faithfully alert and argumentatively ready, and after the three years expired, when reappointment was necessary, the organised workers re-elected Mr. Samuel Smith, with an almost unanimous vote.

Mr. M'Gowan, the Parliamentary Leader of the Labor Party,

is at present actively engaged in combating the Plutocrats in power, and at the next election the Labor Party stand a fair chance of a majority.

THE WEST AUSTRALIAN LABOR PARTY

came into power just a year ago when out of a total of 50 members, composing the Legislative Assembly, 22 were pledged Labor Men, being the strongest party in the House, the Parliamentary Leader of the Labor Party, Mr. Daglish, was sent for and he forthwith formed a Labor Ministry, himself becoming Premier. Whatever may be said as to the Socialistic value of what has taken place, beyond question it must be admitted that the last election in WA which returned these Labor Men represented the class struggle as it was understood, and both Capitalist factions, ex-premier James and his party particularly, did their utmost to maintain the Plutocratic dominancy. If it be said that not very much has been achieved by the Labor Ministry, it can at any rate be said, that whilst for the first time in the history of Parliaments, an avowed Labor Government has occupied office for a year, the heavens have not fallen nor has the sea dried up. Changes have recently taken place in the WA Ministry that indicate unrest, but come what will, there is the fact which nothing can ever wipe out. The defeated ex-premier who represented the bourgeoisie is now in London as Agent General, appointed by the Labor Ministry that defeated him and his Party at the polls and in Parliament. A few more such strides and what will become of the poor old Plutocracy? Really the outlook for the Monopolists is not a promising one, unless indeed their spirit of citizenship enables them to rise higher than their mere sectional interests.

At the Easter Conference of the Labor Party of Victoria, it was decided to definitely declare in favour of Socialism. All who join the Labor Party will now know exactly what the ultimate object aimed at is, and it is much better that it should be so than that the programme should be indefinite and liable to several interpretations. The growth of the Labor Party in the State during the past two years is unprecedented. At that time there were but fourteen Labor Men in a Legislative Assembly of ninety-five members, in the present House there are eighteen members returned on the straight out Labor ticket, in a House of sixty-eight.

THE PARLIAMENTARY LEADER OF THE LABOR PARTY, MR. G. M. PRENDERGAST

has the confidence and hearty support not only of the Labor members but of the Labor Party throughout the whole State. Many of the Branches of the Political Labor Council are systematically engaged in educational and propagandist work. Nowhere in Australia is there more genuine effort put forth to spread sound economic knowledge, and to organise in a business-like fashion. The return of straight out men for Ballarat, Bendigo, Grenville, Geelong and Maryborough is a good indication of what to hope for next Federal Election. At present, Victoria does not return anything like a reasonable proportion of straight-out members to the Federal Parliament; New South Wales returns seven Representatives, Messrs. J. C. Watson, Watkins, Brown, Spence, Webster, Thomas and Hughes; Queensland returns seven Representatives, Messrs. Bamford, Page, MacDonald, Culpin, Thompson, Fisher and Wilkinson; West Australia four Labor Representatives, Messrs. Fowler, Mahon, Carpenter, and Fraser; South Australia three Representatives, Messrs. Batchelor, Poynton and Hutcheson; Victoria three, Messrs. Frank Tudor, Ronald and Dr. Maloney; Tasmania one, King O'Malley. To the Senate, the Queenslanders have returned five out of the six, Messrs. Higgs, Dawson, Stewart, Hurley and Givens; West Australia four, Messrs. Pierce, DeLargie, Croft and Henderson; South Australia, Messrs. McGregor, Guthrie and Storey; Tasmania one, Senator O'Keefe; and Victoria one, Senator Ed. Findley.

Thus there is room for considerable improvement in Victoria yet, and every branch of the Political Labor Council should be preparing for the coming struggle, not merely holding meetings but giving systematic attention to their respective electorates, finding out weaknesses and remedying same. That the fight will be hot is certain, so much the better, that there will be electioneering ability on our opponents side is also a certainty, but all this can be overcome by that whole-souled devotion to a cause which those who belong to the Workers Party can show.

Tasmania has made a fair start with Labor men in the State House; the West Coast did exceptionally well in returning comrades G. N. Burns, Long, and Lammerton, and the workers are gaining ground in the small State as well as elsewhere.

It should be a valuable lesson to those who favour anything less than the clear declaration of Independence from all orthodox parties, no matter how kindly considerate they may be for a time, to find that

THE INDUSTRIALLY ORGANISED WORKERS OF NEW ZEALAND

are organising on purely independent political lines. Those who have, as many Labor men have, held the view that New Zealand is in a satisfactory condition from a Labor standpoint, must indeed be content with very little if they know the facts. There is and always has been a dominant Plutocracy in New Zealand as well as elsewhere, but a few of them in the New Zealand Parliament were shrewd enough to get a little in advance of the ordinary Plutocrats and to pose as advanced Democrats; from the Socialist standpoint the conditions in New Zealand are far from satisfactory. When did any representative group in the New Zealand Parliament or out of it, ever declare in favour of a policy that would put a stop to private rent receiving, interest taking, and profit making? Never. When did the New Zealanders declare in favour of putting a stop to exploitation? Never, except the Socialists who have been trying to organise entirely apart from any of the orthodox politicians. The Arbitration Act has worked well, and is working well. The Factories Act is good for those covered by it. The Land Act is a little in advance of other States, but from the standpoint of enabling the people to become the complete controllers of their own industrial destiny, that certainly is not contemplated by any legislation yet passed or attempted. So it is satisfactory to learn that special efforts are now being put forth to organise a straight-out political Labor Party aiming at Socialism, they are only in their infancy yet, and have yet to win their spurs; but it will come, and ere long we may hope to find the New Zealanders co-operating with those of the Commonwealth, and definitely taking concerted organised action with their fellow workers of other countries; and this brings me to deal briefly with

THE INTERNATIONAL CONGRESSES OF THE WORKERS,

generally held triennially, with which it is not only desirable but urgently necessary that Australia should be properly related. Every student of Sociology that has obtained a correct idea of the historical development of humanity, through Slavery, Serfdom, and Wagedom or Capitalism, and who understands how Universal Capitalism is to-day, knows also that however much patriotism is held up as a virtue by Plutocratic Politicians and a Capitalist press, that Capitalism is absolutely International and recognises no frontiers or boundaries. The financial monopolists are ever seeking additional opportunities for investment, and they have no scruple whatever as to whether the people of any given country are white, brown, yellow or black, providing only they see a chance to get interest; they mind not at all as to what the relationship of the various nations may be; they never allow such considerations to interfere with business, that is, their own private interests. The Capitalists of each country are in actual and active sympathy with each other, and no racial antagonisms prevent concerted action when necessary.

It requires but little education to show how urgently necessary it is that the workers should be equally cosmopolitan. Europeans, Americans and Australasians are all covered by the same economic forces, are all subject to the same guiding tyranny of the Plutocracy, and therefore their interests are absolutely identical. The recognition of this fact has resulted in the organised workers of the world who aim at the realisation of Socialism by constitutional action, holding International Congresses, as a rule triennially, though sometimes they are four years apart. The last of these Congresses was held in September of last year in Amsterdam, Holland, and was attended by 482 delegates from twenty-one Nations. The largest contingent was the British, consisting of 101, the French coming next with 80 and the Germans next with 70 delegates. Such numbers serve to indicate the importance attached to these Congresses by the respective Nations. Australia had one representative, Com. Thompson, of WA; but no proper instructions were given him although he had credentials, as the Labor parties of Australia had not themselves given attention to the matter.

Those individuals that have given the subject attention well know that

SUBJECTS OF THE GREATEST MOMENT TO THE RESPECTIVE PARTIES

of the various countries are discussed at these Congresses as they can be under no other set of circumstances. The next International Congress is fixed to be held in Stuttgart, Germany, in 1907. It is of the greatest importance that the

Australian Labor Party or Parties should be adequately represented at that Congress by delegates properly instructed by those whom they are to represent.

The first step to be taken in connection with this matter is the preparation of a comprehensive report of the social political and economic conditions in Australia, which after preparation and endorsement should be printed in suitable form for presentation to the Congress delegates. It is desirable that all such reports should be prepared and issued and supplied to the secretary of the International Bureau several months before the Congress is held, that the same may be placed in the proper hands early enough. There is therefore ample time to take the matter in hand and deal with the same effectively. Let us hope that the responsible persons will take due note of this, and not allow time to slip by till it is too late.

RELIGION AND MARRIAGE

In view of the criticisms passed upon Socialism recently, it is necessary to remind all, that Socialists base their attitude upon the scientific interpretation of History, and this applies to all departments of knowledge, and serves as a guide for all forms of conduct. Over against the attitude until recently strongly declared by all the churches that all truly devout persons must accept and believe the same, viz: that the World was brought into existence out of nothing 4,004 BC, that man was then made perfect, but fell from his lofty condition, that all other animals were made at the same time, and 'the heavens and all that therein is,' Science teaches that mankind did not begin existence 4,004 BC, but hundreds of thousands of years before; that instead of having made a grand new start as a perfect being and then being cursed by the Creator, there is an abundance of indisputable evidence to show that man began life in so low a condition that it took him many ages even to develop the capacity to rise from all fours and stand on two legs, and very many centuries after that before he was able to develop rationality in any degree. No man of intelligence objects to this to-day, and therefore the Church has accepted the inevitable and endorses what it formerly denied. The orthodox formerly avowed and taught that the oceans of the world and the land and the minerals were brought into existence in six ordinary days. Science has demonstrated that the earth and all the other planets of the Solar system were at one time in a gaseous form, and in the course of myriads of centuries have cooled down and so been in a state of continual change and as a result we have the minerals, the rocks, the land, and the water, salt and fresh, and everything that has ever dwelt upon the earth or that does now dwell thereon has been and is now subject to the same law of change or development; and only the ignorant ever think of taking exception to this view.

IT IS THE LAW OF PROGRESS

and the theologians no longer oppose such well established facts, but they did with all their might, and declared that all who said otherwise were grossly irreligious. As though it were wrong to develop the understanding, as though it were wicked to train the intellect and to study the wonders of nature and so gradually substitute intelligence for ignorance. Many honest-minded men and women have been miserable beyond endurance because they wished to be truly religious, and yet found many things in connection with religion as they had been taught it, outrageously cruel, mean, and degrading. The degrading ceremonies of the ancient Jews as recorded in the Bible can easily be understood when it is remembered that they were only a semi-civilised people believing in the gross superstitions and resorting to the barbarous behaviour of semi-savages, gradually working their way from savagery and barbarism to civilised life, and of course like all other peoples learning by myriads of experiences how to develop the worthier side at the expense of the baser. So one can not only make allowance for their barbarities, but can see a strong confirmation of the evolutionary theory of human as well as all other development. Yet when Charles Darwin, the Biologist, in his epoch making works 'The Origin of Species' and 'The Descent of Man,' adduced evidence to prove the development of man from lower forms, he was vehemently assailed on all sides by the clericals, preached at, denounced, condemned, vilified, classed as atheist, &c. Darwin's great crime consisting of contributing to the world's knowledge, as the result of many years of devoted study. To-day, Darwin's name and that of his co-workers, Professors Alfred Russell Wallace, Tyndall, Huxley, Lyell, &c., &c., stand revered the world over as master minds in their respective departments, but of course, as none taught more strongly than they, knowledge must be constantly added to as the result of constant study, with the ever-developing faculties of a growing humanity, and so, as knowledge is increased ideas and opinions change and always for the better, because always as the result of a fuller understanding of nature's laws, including ourselves. This is what is meant by

THE SCIENTIFIC INTERPRETATION OF HISTORY,

cheerfully recognising the universal law of continuous progression, and the consequent moulding of conduct that this entails. This is the bed rock upon which all Scientific Socialists rest their case, and they need no other. Therefore one can dwell upon the marvellous work of the Omnipotent and Omniscient, can reverentially dwell upon the ever unfolding of the mysteries of the universe, can rejoice that it is permitted to us to add wondrously to our stock of knowledge by such aids as the spectroscope, telescope, microscope, to be able to measure the distances of the celestial bodies, to gauge their size, to weigh their mass, to analyse their composition, to waft messages thousands of miles by wireless telegraphy, all tells of knowledge acquired and applied by man in his march towards a possible perfection. Moses did the best he could as a teacher and guide, and for his day doubtless he did exceeding well; but is humanity not to progress after Moses or any other teacher? And are those who teach ever to be denounced as sacrilegious and unworthy innovators? Yes, it would appear that it is so difficult for some of us to change opinions and bring ourselves into line with the truest knowledge that being impelled to say something, we find it easier to condemn what we cannot understand and therefore we begin to denounce the more worthy. But this really does not matter, as the pioneers of knowledge know how hard it was for them at one time to become diligent students instead of being content with the conditions they were born in.

As in other departments of knowledge, so in Sociological affairs, or the affairs directly affecting human life. The student knows that the forms of human society have been such as were necessary for the particular kind of development at each stage of progress. Naturally some sections are mentally and morally in advance of their fellows, and experience the limitations and faultinesses of any given system prior to their fellows, and some of these advocate the desirability of a change, and the kind of change desired is always one that shall admit of humanity developing a few degrees more perfectly than the existing conditions allow of. So in passing through

THE TRIBAL STAGE, CHATTEL SLAVERY, AND SERFDOM,

and now in passing through Wagedom or Capitalism, it is found that all civilised society is relatively rapidly getting to think more and more of the community and less of self and one's own family; *i.e.* not that they become disregardent of the individual and the family, but manifest increasing concern for the welfare of each family and each individual by true concern for the community as a whole.

The Patriarchal Family was complete, with the Father, who was master and owner of each and all and everything. The persons and the chattels were his property. Humanity has travelled beyond the stage when that ownership of persons in the patriarchal fashion can serve completely the requirements of modern life, and therefore we see the foundations of patriarchal family life in process of change. It is still the unit, but not anything like it was under the true patriarchal *regime*; not only was the woman not allowed to have a voice and a vote in worldly affairs, she was the slave of the man, to do his bidding unquestioningly, and the prevalent religious forms pronounced their blessing upon such relations. They doubtless met the requirements of certain times, that such conditions do not suit modern necessities is known to everybody: and so already, marriage has become a civil contract and women have claimed and obtained the right to vote as free and independent citizens, quite irrespective of the opinions of men folk, even of those of their own household. This is so marked a departure, so contrary to the Patriarchal principle, that still further modifications may be expected to follow. In what direction there does not appear to be any general agreement, except for this, that all Socialists having made a special study of the causes that retard human development are strongly in favour of economic, or industrial and social freedom for women, the same as for men, by which is meant that all human beings, men and women alike, should be educated and trained, qualified and enabled to obtain all the essentials of a full free and healthy life. Therefore the agitation on behalf of the Labor Parties, for

EQUAL PAY, FOR EQUAL WORK, FOR WOMEN AND MEN.

Women must not be condemned to an inferior standard of social well-being because they happen not to be married, and young women living at their own homes should not be encouraged to accept as wages a nominal sum altogether unequal to their adequate maintenance, if for similar work young men would be entitled to a fuller share. It is not kindness on the part of parents to take up the position that if the girls can get what will keep them in clothing &c., they may live at home and share with the family; to do this is to encourage the worst forms of sweating. It may be that workmen's families buy commodities at a lower price than would be possible if such young women did not work for less than half the proper remuneration, that in no way mitigates the evil, its effects are blasting. Of course, if such young women get married pretty early, the evil effects are not so pronounced in their cases, but when as under existing conditions is always the case, a high percentage does not marry early, they are themselves deprived of opportunities which ought to be theirs, and which, if they were not treated as inferior beings would be theirs. I will not enter into a discussion or description of the glaring evils arising in consequence of the abnormal and artificial sexual relations that arise in every country in consequence of this economic handicapping of women, but no one with any knowledge of existing conditions can express satisfaction therewith.

Why have the Australians decided in favour of the political emancipation of women, if it is not that they may use political power to bring about social and industrial changes, and therefore in favour of economic freedom?

Is there any good in men or women having political power unless it be used to alter the social surroundings from an unsatisfactory state to a satisfactory state? Certainly it would be a mockery to say to any, 'you may have political power but you must not use it.' Or, 'you are entrusted with the power to vote but you must vote as we decide,' or, 'political power must not be used to raise the standard of life:' It is too late for any to take up such an attitude now. The reactionaries will do so, because it is 'their nature to,' but that will have no effect upon the possessors of political power.

Dealing with this subject by

A LETTER TO THE MELBOURNE 'ARGUS'

two years ago, I then wrote, 'As to the effect of Socialism on family life, the present system absolutely forbids the possibility of family life to a very large proportion of the community. Every one knows that in each of these Australasian States, including New Zealand, family life is quite impossible for such a large number, that not only is there a serious decline in what should be the natural increase of the population, but which has led to other evils of so grave a character as to give most serious concern to all well-wishers of the community.

The present marriage system is based upon the supposition of economic dependence of the woman on the man, and, as a result, sex domination obtains. Political freedom will, we hope, result in economic freedom for both sexes alike. The country that has already politically enfranchised women, must prepare itself for the broader issue.'

Considerable criticism has been passed upon the above statement, I adhere to every word of it, and it stands perfectly unassailable, as it merely indicates the present trend of politico-economic affairs, not in Australia only but throughout civilisation.

The following extract is from the very able and lengthy article on Socialism in the 'Encyclopedia Britannica.' 'On Religion as on Marriage, Socialism has no special teaching, The Social Democrats of Germany in their Gotha programme of 1875, declare religion to be a private concern. As we have seen Christian Socialism is a considerable force in many European countries, and in many of the other schools, especially that of Louis Blanc, the kinship and even identity of ethical spirit with that of Christianity, are unmistakeable.'

HOW TO ESTIMATE VALUES UNDER SOCIALISM

The question of values and how to estimate the value of services under a Socialist regime, is often dwelt upon, the following brief statement on this subject from Dr. Karl Marx's 'Capital' is helpful. 'Some might think that if the value of a commodity is determined by the quantity of labour spent on it, the more idle and unskilful the labourer, the more valuable would his commodity be, because more time would be required in its production. The labour, however, that forms the substance of value, is homogeneous labour, expenditure of one uniform labour-power. The total labour-power of society, which is embodied in the sum total of the values of all commodities produced by that society, counts here as one homogeneous mass of human labour-power, composed though it be of innumerable individual units.

Each of these units is the same as any other so far as it has the character of the average labour-power of society, and takes effect as such; that is, so far as it requires for producing a commodity, no more time than is needed on an average, no more than is socially necessary.'

SOCIALISM AND COMMUNISM

It is a common thing for some to speak very favourably of Socialism, and very unfavourably of Communism, this arises mainly in consequence of lack of knowledge as to what Communism is. It is the full realisation of the Collectivist ideal, when not only will the means of wealth production be cooperatively owned by the people, but when there will be no regimentation or any dictatorial official class of the kind we have knowledge of to-day, when even Parliaments will disappear very largely if not wholly. Socialists desire a free State of society wherein exploitation will be impossible and minus armies of officials or Parliamentarians.

For a Socialist to declare, imply or tolerate the idea that Socialism is sound, economically and ethically but that Communism is unsound is preposterous. When Capitalism is superseded by Socialism, influence will begin to operate favourable to the shedding of officials and permanent politicians, and Society will doubtless travel to Communism. Only those who have not thought the subject out will have any hesitancy in accepting this, but when it is realised that it would be as illogical to suppose Society will not continue to develop beyond Socialism, as it would be now to declare it cannot go beyond Capitalism, the absurdity of it will be seen and dropped.

The following extract from a Lecture by the late William Morris, author of 'Earthly Paradise' and very many other works, is worthy of attention, he says there are 'two views taken among Socialists as to the future of society, according to the first, the State – that is, the Nation organised for unwasteful production and exchange of wealth – will be the sole possessor of the national plant and stock, the sole employer of labour, which she will so regulate in the general interest that no man will ever need to fear lack of employment and due earnings therefrom. Everybody will have an equal chance of livelihood, and, except as a rare disease there would be no hoarding of money or other wealth. This view points to an attempt to give everybody the full worth of the productive work done by him, after having ensured the necessary preliminary that he shall always be free to work.

According to the other view,

THE CENTRALISED NATION WOULD GIVE PLACE TO A FEDERATION OF COMMUNITIES

who would hold all wealth in common, and would use that wealth for satisfying the needs of each member, only exacting from each that he should do his best according to his capacity towards the production of the commonwealth. Of course, it is to be understood that each member is absolutely free to use his share of wealth as he pleases, without interference from any, so long as he really uses it, that is, does not turn it into an instrument for the oppression of others. This view intends complete equality of condition for every one, though life would be, as always, varied by the differences of capacity and disposition; and emulation in working for the common good would supply the place of competition as an incentive.

These two views of the future of Society are sometimes opposed to each other as Socialism and Communism; but to my mind the latter is simply the necessary development of the former, which implies a transition period, during which people would be getting rid of the habits of mind bred by the long ages of tyranny and commercial competition, and be learning that it is to the interest of each that all should thrive.' The preceding quotation is from a Lecture by William Morris, delivered in Edinburgh in 1886, one of a series of six from as many representative men, including the grand old Socialist and Social Reformer, the author of 'The Wonderful Century,' Professor Alfred Russell Wallace, compeer and co-worker with Chas. Darwin. Professor Wallace is a Socialist and profoundly religious, take any of his works on Social Reforms or any of his works dealing with spiritual matters and always there is the same loving heart and wise head presenting knowledge and showing sympathy not only with the suffering but with those at work as Social Reformers.

Most readers will have seen statements from

MEN WHO ARE YOUNG IN THE SOCIALIST MOVEMENT

who declare they have sympathy with Socialism, but not with the Socialism of the Continent of Europe. This is simply because they lack knowledge. It is as though someone should say, I believe in Capitalism but not in the Capitalism of England or America. Just as the Capitalist system is found most highly developed in the countries named so has Socialism been scientifically studied and elaborated in all its bearings on the Continent of Europe. To think of endorsing Socialism and not to endorse the Socialism of Europe would be more ludicrous than to attempt the play of Hamlet, leaving the Danish prince out. Indeed such admissions are only made by ill-informed persons who are at the mercy of critics, oftentimes knowing no better than themselves, but unscrupulous and mercenary, writing under cover of the Capitalist press.

However, it is easy for those who are willing to take the trouble to know exactly what are the principles and what the policy of Socialists of the respective European peoples. Two years ago there appeared a volume entitled MODERN SOCIALISM, edited by R. C. K. Ensor, published by Harper Bros., London. This volume contains not only speeches by representative men in the Socialist movement, but gives also the statement of Principles and actual programmes of the respective parties. The cost of the work is six shillings; its value cannot be overrated. The Programmes of the German, Austrian, Belgian, French and British Parties are given, and reports of Lectures or Speeches of representative persons of many countries, making up a volume that may well serve as a guide to all students.

In order that those who have thought the Continental Socialists are a wild sort of folk, not knowing what citizenship means, or finding pleasure in some outrageous demands, I transfer from the book named, the statement of principles by the German Social Democratic Party that precedes their actual programme. And as everyone knows the Germans are the most perfectly organised of the Socialists of the world, and may be quoted as being in the forefront of Socialist organisations.

'The economic development of bourgeois society leads by natural necessity to the downfall of the small industry, whose foundation is formed by the worker's private ownership of his means of production. It separates the worker from his means of production, and converts him into a propertyless proletarian, while the means of production become the monopoly of a relatively small number of capitalists and large landowners.

HAND-IN-HAND WITH THIS MONOPOLISATION OF THE MEANS OF PRODUCTION

goes the displacement of the dispersed small industries by colossal great industries, the development of the tool into the machine, and a gigantic growth in the productivity of human labour. But all the advantages of this transformation are monopolised by capitalists and large landowners. For the proletariat and the declining intermediate classes – petty bourgeoisie and peasants – it means a growing augmentation of the insecurity of their existence, of misery, oppression, enslavement, debasement, and exploitation.

Ever greater grows the number of proletarians, ever more enormous the army of surplus workers, ever sharper the oppression between exploiters and exploited, ever bitterer the class-war between bourgeoisie and proletariat, which divides modern society into two hostile camps, and is the common hall-mark of all industrial countries.

The gulf between the propertied and the propertyless is further widened through the crises, founded in the essence of the capitalistic method of production, which constantly become more comprehensive and more devastating, which elevate general insecurity to the normal condition of society, and which prove that the powers of production of contemporary society have grown beyond measure, and that private ownership of the means of production has become incompatible with their application to their objects and their full development.

Private ownership of the means of production, which was formerly the means of securing to the producer the ownership of his product, has to-day become the means of expropriating peasants, manual workers, and small traders, and enabling the non-workers – capitalists and large landowners – to own the product of the workers. Only the transformation of capitalistic private ownership of the means of production – the soil, mines, raw materials, tools, machines, and means of transport – into social ownership, and the transformation of production of goods for sale into Socialistic production, managed for and through society, can bring it about, that the great industry and the steadily growing productive capacity of social labour shall for the hitherto exploited classes be changed from a source of misery and oppression, to a source of the highest welfare and of all-round harmonious perfection.

This social transformation means the emancipation not only of the proletariat, but of the whole human race which suffers under the conditions to-day. But it can only be the work of the working class, because all the other classes, in spite of mutually conflicting interests, take their stand on

THE BASIS OF PRIVATE OWNERSHIP OF THE MEANS OF PRODUCTION,

and have as their common object the preservation of the principles of contemporary society.

The battle of the working-class against Capitalist exploitation is necessarily a political battle. The working-class cannot carry on its economic battles or develop its economic organisation without political rights. It cannot effect the passing of the means of production into the ownership of the community without acquiring political power.

To shape this battle of the working-class into a conscious and united effort, and to show it its naturally necessary end is the object of the Social Democratic Party.

The interests of the working-class are the same in all lands with capitalistic methods of production. With the expansion of world-transport and production for the world-market, the state of the workers in any one country becomes constantly more dependent on the state of the workers in other countries. The emancipation of the working-class is thus a task in which the workers of all civilised countries are concerned in a like degree. Conscious of this, the Social Democratic Party of Germany feels and declares itself *one* with the class-conscious workers of all other lands.

The Social Democratic Party of Germany fights thus not for new class privileges and exceptional rights, but for the abolition of class-domination and of the classes themselves, and for the equal rights and equal obligations of all, without distinction of sex and parentage. Setting out from these views, it combats in contemporary society not merely the exploitation and oppression of the wage-workers, but every kind of exploitation and oppression, whether directed against a class, a party, a sex, or a race.'

This statement of principles is followed by the immediate demands of the party, and which want of space alone precludes insertion, but from the statement given may be gathered the entire *raison d'être* of the Socialist movement, not a sentence too much or too little, and each country in turn presents its case with equally correct economic reasoning. No other political party in any country does anything of the kind:

WHICH OF THE PLUTOCRATIC PARTIES DARES ATTEMPT

to analyse society equally scientifically? Not one! the very attempt would again prove how unnecessary they were to the world. Socialists themselves will do well to carefully study this German statement, as brief though it is all salient features are dwelt upon. That statement was agreed upon at the Erfurt Conference of the party, in 1891, and has been ratified at each of their subsequent Congresses. In the same year the Austrian Social Democratic Party held their Congress at Brunn, and their statement preceding their programme is in all essentials like that of the German, just as a sample I give the first paragraph: 'The Social Democratic Labour Party in Austria strives on behalf of the whole people without distinction of nation, race, or sex, for emancipation from the fetters of economic dependence, political oppression, and intellectual confinement. The cause of these unsatisfactory conditions lies, not in particular political arrangements, but in the fact essentially conditioning and dominating the whole state of society, that the means of working are monopolised in the hands of individual possessors. The possessors of the power to work, the working-class, fall therefore into the most oppressive dependence upon the possessors of the means of working which include land – that is, upon the great land-owning and capitalistic classes, whose political and economic domination is expressed in the class state of to-day.'

Thus, having diagnosed scientifically the causes of exploitation and its results, the Austrians declare in favour of 'an international party; it condemns the privileges of nations as well as those of birth and sex, property and lineage, and declares that the war against exploitation must be international like the exploitation itself.'

Equally interesting and educative is the statement of principles of the 'French Socialist Party,' voted upon and accepted at Tours, in March 1902. A couple of paragraphs will prove interesting. Say the French – 'Proletarians are acknowledged as fit citizens to manage the milliards of the national and communal budgets; (i.e. the finances of the local governing bodies) as labourers in the workshop, they are only a passive multitude, which has no share in the direction of enterprises, and

THEY ENDURE THE DOMINATION OF A CLASS

which makes them pay dearly for a tutelage whose utility ceases and whose prolongation is arbitrary.

The irresistible tendency of the proletarians, therefore, is to transfer into the economic order the democracy partially realised in the political order. Just as all the citizens have and handle in common, democratically, the political power, so they must have and handle in common the economic power, the means of production.' This should go far to satisfy those who have thought that Socialists could not agree as to what Socialism is, the fact being, there is no disagreement, as to main essentials or as to policy, and very little as to method.

The oldest of the Socialist's bodies in England is the Social Democratic Federation formed in 1883, this organisation also issues its statement of principles which are so like those of the continent, that it would be superfluous to quote at length. It is well, however, to give proof of the oneness of aim and agreement as to necessity; therefore, says the SDF. 'The economic development of modern society is characterised by the more or less complete domination of the Capitalistic mode of production, over all branches of human labour.

The capitalistic mode of production, because it has the creation of profit for its sole object, therefore favours the larger capital, and is based upon the divorcement of the majority of the people from the instruments of production and the concentration of these instruments in the hands of a minority. Society is thus divided into two opposite classes, one, the capitalists and their sleeping partners, the landlords and loanmongers, holding in their hands the means of production, distribution, and exchange, and being, therefore, able to command the labour of others; the other, the working-class, the wage-earners, the proletariat, possessing nothing but their labour-power, and being consequently forced by necessity to work for the former.'

Thus it will be seen there is an agreement in every country as to what Socialism is, and why it is inevitable.

THE SOCIALISTS OF RUSSIA AND OF JAPAN

equally agree in the principle of a common brotherhood based on 'The Socialization of the means of production, Distribution, and Exchange, to be controlled by a Democratic State in the interests of the entire community, and the complete emancipation of Labour from the Domination of Capitalism and Landlordism, with the establishment of Social and Economic Equality between the Sexes.' – English SDF object.

In addition to the Social Democratic Federation of Great Britain, there is another Socialist body. The Independent Labour Party, whose activity is very considerable and who

conduct a systematic propaganda continuously throughout the
UK their object is pithily put: 'An industrial Commonwealth
founded upon the Socialization of Land and Capital.' The
reasons for this are given as, 'The true object of industry being
the production of the requirements of life, the responsibility
should rest with the community collectively, therefore. The
land, being the storehouse of all the necessaries of life, should
be declared and treated as public property. The capital
necessary for industrial operations should be owned and used
collectively. Work and wealth resulting therefrom, should be
equitably distributed over the population.'

Then follows the programme.

Both the SDF and the ILP together with the Fabian Society
have done very much educational work, and it has resulted in
the formation of a much larger third body or organisation
known as the Labour Representation Committee, now five
years old, formed really out of and by the Trade Union
Congress, in order to give all necessary attention to the desires
of the workers from the political standpoint as expressed by the
parent body. The first essential condition of this new political
organisation was, that it was to be entirely independent of, and
apart from the bourgeois, or orthodox political parties of the
day. It was not to be Conservative, Liberal or Radical, or be in
anyway identified with these bodies, but straight-out 'Labour.'
It was not declared to be Socialist, on the contrary, when an
effort was made that the declared objective of the new body
should be the realisation of Socialism, the majority of delegates
declared it was unnecessary to make any such declaration;
what was wanted said they, was the bringing together of the
Trade Unionist and Socialist forces; and it appears they have
succeeded. At the LRC Conference this year

THE SOCIALIST OBJECTIVE WAS EASILY CARRIED,

and this represents a million of the organised workers. This
may be taken as a decisive indication of the development of
affairs in the UK as the most perfectly organised bodies of
workers are directly connected with, and are largely
responsible for the movement. About seventy Socialist and
Labour Candidates are prepared to take the field immediately
there are signs of a general election, and of these about forty
will be returned, so that after the next election the House of
Commons will at least have a group of straight-out fellows to
sturdily fight the workers cause.

As bearing upon the pledge signing by candidates which has received some public attention here, it is interesting to note that the LRC is quite definite on the matter. The following is the declared immediate object of the organisation:—

'To secure, by united action, the election to Parliament of candidates promoted, in the first instance, by an affiliated society or societies in the constituency, who undertake to form or join a distinct group in Parliament with its own whips and its own policy on labour questions, to abstain strictly from identifying themselves with or promoting the interests of any section of the Liberal or Conservative parties, and not to oppose any other candidate recognised by this committee. All such candidates shall pledge themselves to accept this constitution, or resign, and to appear before their constituencies under the title of Labour Candidates only.'

LABOR'S ADVANCING ARMY

Most of the information given below is based on material issued by the Secretary of the International Social Bureau; but at the time it was issued it was not known to the Bureau that Labor Candidates in Australia stood on a definite Socialist basis and therefore they were not included. After what has taken place at the respective State Congresses or Conventions, and the endorsement of the Socialist objective by the Interstate Labor Conference, held in Melbourne, July 1905, no one could give an account of the Socialist representatives in the various Parliaments, and on Municipal bodies, without including the Australian Labor Men, but to guard against criticism, I admit it would not be right to declare that all are definitely Socialist, it can only be said of some of them that they are Socialistic in trend, but no one can doubt that the

GUIDING OR DRIVING FORCE IS SOCIALISM PURE AND SIMPLE,

and the same now applies to the Socialist and Labour members returned in the United Kingdom, Labour only though some of them are, they are consciously or otherwise, the evidence of the antagonism of classes brought about by modern Capitalism.

At the Federal Election in December 1903, the Labor Party ran Candidates for the Senate in each State, including Tasmania. By taking the highest vote in each State recorded for Labor-Senate Candidates, we get the total of 321,225; the number returned in the above list stands for Representatives.

SOCIALIST AND LABOR REPRESENTATIVES, AND THE LABOR–SOCIALIST VOTE OF THE WORLD

	Year of election	Vote	Labor–Socialists elected including by-elections	Total Repre- sentatives
Germany	1903	3,010,472	83	397
France	1902	805,000	49	584
Austria	1901	780,000	10	363
Belgium	1904	463,967	28	166
Italy	1904	301,525	29	508
United Kingdom	1902	150,000	13	670
Switzerland	1902	100,000	6	145
Australia	1903	321,225	25	75
United States	1904	600,000	–	–
Denmark	1903	53,479	16	102
Holland	1902	38,279	7	100
Norway	1903	30,000	4	114
Spain	1903	29,000	–	–
Sweden	1902	10,000	4	230
Bulgaria	1903	9,000	–	–
Canada	1903	8,025	–	–
Argentina	1903	5,000	1	–

There is probably no other country in the world where so general an opportunity was afforded to test the feeling, as for Senate purposes, each State forms one electorate and therefore the vote recorded is not for a portion of Australia, but literally for the whole of the Commonwealth, women as well as men.

One half of the Senators and Representatives retired and were eligible for re-election at the last election, so the number of Senators and of Representatives is composed of those who were returned at the last two elections.

The total number of Labor Senators is fourteen out of a total of thirty-six, there being a total of six Senators for each State, irrespective of the population.

QUEENSLAND HEADS THE LIST

with five Labor men out of six possible as follows:

Queensland. – Labor Senators: Senators Higgs, Dawson, Stewart, Turley, Givens   5

Western Australia: Senators Pierce, DeLargie, Henderson, and Croft   4

South Australia: Senators McGregor, Guthrie, and Storey   3

Victoria: Senator Ed. Findley   1

Tasmania: Senator O'Keefe   1

THE FEDERAL HOUSE OF REPRESENTATIVES
consists of 75 members, as follows:

State	Labor Members	Total Reps.
New South Wales	7	27
Victoria	3	22
South Australia	3	7
Queensland	7	9
West Australia	4	5
Tasmania	1	5
	—	—
	25	75

STATE ASSEMBLIES

	Labor Members	Total
New South Wales	23	90
Victoria	18	68
South Australia	15	42
Western Australia	22	50
Queensland	35	72
Tasmania	4	38
	—	—
	117	360

LABOUR AND SOCIALIST MAYORS, ALDERMEN, COUNCILLORS, GUARDIANS, ETC.

Germany	111	Representatives in different State Diets
United Kingdom	790	Aldermen, County, Town, and Urban District Councillors and Members of Boards of Guardians.
France	68	Mayors,
	1200	Municipal Councillors,
	43	Provincial Councillors.
Italy	100	Municipal Councils in hands of the Socialists.
Belgium	600	Municipal Councillors,
	70	Provincial Councillors,
	4	Senators.
Denmark	400	Municipal Councillors,
	1	Senator.
Sweden	20	Municipal Councillors.
Norway	17	Municipal Councillors.
Switzerland	—	The Socialist Party is represented in 17 Cantons and
	41	Municipal Councillors in 178 Municipalities.
United States	350	Socialists on various Public Bodies.

This is not a bad start, and now the respective Plutocratic parties are merging their forces to make common cause against the Socialists. This must come; all pretence of having real sympathy with Socialist aspirations will be dropped by the reactionaries as soon as the respective forces get to close quarters. I know full well the tendency on the part of some well-meaning comrades to appear always as models of decorum, harbingers of peace, ultra respectable, no opposition to anyone or anything; I know also how utterly futile they are and must be to accomplish anything of value. The fight has begun but it is by no means over, and those who have no understanding that it is a real struggle we are engaged in are of very little use to the movement.

Whilst children are dying by hundreds of thousands, women groaning because they cannot command life's necessaries for their children, and millions of men in the respective countries barred by unemployment from getting life's necessaries, and this in the midst of a superfluity of wealth the like of which the world has never known before,

THE CLARION CRY GOES FORTH TO ALL

vigorously appealing to every true comrade to get to work and achieve something. Never before in History so far as we have knowledge has there been such a universality of expectancy. The times are ripe for great changes, those changes are certain to come, not the mere pettifogging changes of fiscalism, not the trifling additions to wages, brought about now and again for some sections by one or other agencies, but definite deep-rooted drastic changes, the de-throning of the monopolists, the people themselves becoming direct owners and controllers of themselves and the wealth they produce; is this not the time to ask for Peace?

Peace between Capital and Labor, is that all you ask?
Is Peace then the only thing needful?
There was Peace enough in Southern slavery.
There is a Peace of life and another of death.
It is well to rise above violence.
It is well to rise superior to anger.
But if peace means final acquiescence in wrong, – if your aim
   is less than justice, and peace, forever one, – then your
   peace is a crime.

ERNEST CROSBY

NEWSPAPERS

	Socialist and Labour Party Papers	Dailies (included in first col.)	Trade Union and Labour Papers
Germany	84	54	75
Italy	69	5	23
France	45	3	—
Belgium	42	6	11
Austria	37	2	55
United Kingdom	6	—	16
Denmark	24	22	32
United States	40	2	—
Holland	12	1	—
Spain	12	—	—
Bulgaria	9	—	—
Australia	6	—	—
Sweden	13	3	—
Norway	6	3	—
Switzerland	5	—	—
Finland	8	1	—
Argentina	2	—	—

The chief cause of the English Workman being so much behind his Continental brother in so many important directions, is traceable to his snobbish notion of respectability. With opportunities exceeding those of workers in any other European Country, so insular and bourgeois, so lacking in class-consciousness has the representative British worker been, that until just recently it seemed next to hopeless to expect any advance.

Even now, how poor by comparison do the British workers show up as evidenced by the lists previously given. Look at the aggregate Socialist vote in the UK, a country with 42 millions of inhabitants – even though the franchise may be faulty – they have seven millions of electors on the rolls, and the workers have a large majority of the votes in 70 per cent of the electorates! How often has the need for a daily paper, owned and entirely controlled by the workers been called for, and how feeble the response! Australians may not be conscious of it but they exhibit the faultiness of the Britisher in many serious respects; To

THINK OF THE INSULTS THAT HAVE BEEN THROWN AT THE LABOR PARTY

by the Plutocratic press, to realise how great a service could be rendered to the cause if the party owned an efficiently conducted daily paper, should be sufficient stimulus to bring one into speedy existence. At last it looks as though a sensible effort is to be made in South Australia and Victoria, perhaps by the time the workers are a little more educated in social economics, the effort will be crowned with success. It is not too much to hope to see during the next few years, not merely more perfected organisation, but also such educational agencies in the hands of the disciplined bodies of workers, that we shall be entirely out of the swaddling clothes stage.

The Socialist Labor Party of Australia should be so perfectly organised and thoroughly equipped that nothing should ever go by default. As yet the literary department is woefully deficient. Every State Party ought to systematically educate the electorate in everything appertaining to the Socialist movement of the world. The weekly Labor papers at present serving as the chief organs, are of course doing the best they can, but how trifling compared to the stupendous work that needs to be accomplished. More weeklies and dailies will be necessary, and it is high time business capacity was shown in this direction.

Without literature of the right sort the workers cannot be properly qualified to discern between the subtleties of political charlatans, who are ever alert to turn aside the movement from the straight path that leads to social ownership of the agencies of production.

How well I know the plausible person who says, 'Really you know I would go as far as necessary but one mustn't go too fast.' And such a person's notion of going fast enough is to follow the crowd even if it drops him through the sands and the mulga because he hasn't the courage or capacity to make one to get the crowd on to the right road. I urge upon my readers, more especially upon the young men, to be at all times most tolerant and kindly towards all who have done good work even on the most superficial plane; but I also urge them not to consider it kindness to hesitate to always declare for straight-out action and go the 'whole hog'.

Remember we are not building a nation of workers to fight some other nation of workers either in a military or an industrial sense.

INDUSTRIAL WARFARE IS FRAUGHT WITH HORRORS

every wit as awful as military or naval warfare. Until now the

workers of each country in turn have been gulled that they are
a wonderfully superior people to the workers of some other
nation. Now we know how absolutely true it is that the
interests of the workers of all lands are perfectly identical.
Future fights must not be between the workers of one country
and the workers of another, that is madness, the fight we are
called upon to engage in is, as part of a disciplined army of
world's workers, battling against the workers' exploiters in
every country alike.

Socialism enjoins International peace and universal good will
amongst all peoples. No other influence known to men has
operated half so powerfully to eradicate racial animosities and
national jealousies. All through the centuries led by the
dominant propertied class in both countries the French and
English have been slaying each other. Of late years this has
given place to incessant industrial warfare; each undermining
the other, the spice for this is found in the profits of the
respective plutocratic sections; for variety, Germans v French,
British v Dutch or Russians and Russians v Japs; but always
tearing each other. As Socialists we have no quarrel with the
workers of any nation on earth. There is ample room for all in
the world, it is only the conducting of industry for the
profit-making purposes of the Plutocracy that makes it appear
each nation must fight every other nation. Stop this, and begin
to produce for use and there is room for all, and work for all
and of course a market for all. With us it is not France v
Germany, or Europe v America, but each for all and all for
each. But to make this possible the exploiters must be got rid
of. We declare a class war to get rid of classes, and ever after to
have a people on the basis of economic equality.

WE PREACH A PEACE

that so far transcends the peace proclaimed by churches, that
whereas, the Churches in each nation back up the murderous
empire extending policy, Socialists always declare in favour of
the solidarity of the interests of the workers of every country.
An American writer has put this so forcibly, and it is always
helpful to study what the Americans, as the most progressive,
are thinking and saying, that it cannot but be interesting to
readers. 'More and more the enlightened proletarian is realising
that war means for him, but continual exploitation and
enslavement. More and more he is learning that every attempt
to exploit the workers of another country only fastens the

shackles of exploitation more firmly upon his own limbs. More and more he is learning that every blow aimed at the interests of the working class of Europe, of Asia, or the far off Isles of the sea, will only rebound with four-fold force upon his own back. More and more he is learning that the irrepressible conflict of to-day is not between the workers of one nation and the workers of another nation, but it is a conflict between the capitalists and the workers of all nations, and so above every appeal to national pride, above every appeal to religious prejudice, above every appeal to race-hatred, sounds high and clear the clarion call of the Socialist movement. 'Workers of all countries, unite! You have the whole world to win and nothing but your chains to lose.'

And back from the hills and valleys of the German fatherland in mighty volume more than three million strong; back from the sunny fields of France, green and peaceful and smiling; back from England, from Belgium, from Spain, from Italy; back from more than six million militant Socialists throughout the civilised world comes the answering cry in the language of that message which was sent by the Berlin comrades to the Paris comrades during the Franco–Prussian conflict: 'We are the enemies of all wars, solemnly we promise that neither the sound of the trumpet nor the roar of the cannon, neither victory nor defeat will swerve us from our common purpose, the union of the children of toil of all countries.' That is the spirit of the working class movement. That is the spirit which above all others is making for human brotherhood and universal peace. This is the spirit of the newer and truer patriotism for the spurious and

BOMBASTIC PATRIOTISM WHICH ARRAYS RACE AGAINST RACE

and nation against nation, which glories in war and finds its highest inspiration in the trumpery of a military parade; for that spurious and bombastic patriotism which glorifies the deeds of our fathers but stultifies every principle for which they fought; for that spurious and bombastic patriotism whose other name is tyranny, oppression, exploitation, capitalism, the world over, we have no use whatever. Against it our whole soul sickens and revolts. But to that newer and truer patriotism which recognises the whole world as my nation and every man as my brother: to that newer and truer patriotism which realises that there is more glory in peace than in war; to that patriotism which would turn our warships into floating hospitals and our tented fields into kindergarten playgrounds; to that truer patriotism whose banner over us is the world-wide red banner of Socialism, not the flag of bloody revolution, but fitting symbol of the fact that one blood courses through the veins of the whole human family; to that newer and truer patriotism whose shibboleth is liberty, fraternity, and equality, and whose other name is justice and peace, for ever one, the working class movement of the world, gives its whole-souled allegiance.' Dr. Howard A. Gibbs, in 'The Comrade', Cooper Square, New York.

How lofty the aspiration and how noble the mental and moral attitude shown in this citation as contrasted with the puny bickerings of orthodox politicians and the mean aims of competitive commercialists. America has been relatively slow to accept and to advocate the necessity for Socialism; there more than elsewhere the gospel of 'getting on' on the most blatant individualist lines was for several generations the ideal – if such it may be termed. From every country in Europe there flocked to America those whose only ambition was 'to make a bit' to 'scoop the pool,' a natural desire on the part of those who had been subjected to old world aristocratic and plutocratic domination, and in turn they exhibited the very worst evils of a bossing gold-hunting exploiting plutocracy, and the world may be grateful not only that the field was afforded them to indulge that propensity, but still more grateful that having passed through the experiment, the educated amongst them are now in the front rank of the world's advocates of a genuine Collectivism. This fact is surely a very weighty one and

WORTHY OF SERIOUS ATTENTION BY AUSTRALIANS

many of whom, who claim to be guides *re* matters of social and industrial reform, have nothing better to offer than a policy of fiscalism, and largely on the grounds that 'America has succeeded so well on it.' The day has gone when it was possible to build up a nation to pass through the experience of America and the older countries, economic development absolutely forbids it; England had a long innings, because the capitalist movement based on machine-made commodities began with her, and slowly (though quickly compared with other economic phases) she developed the Joint Stock

Companies, the Syndicates and Trusts: America picking up the Trusts developed them in every conceivable direction, and rushed through with National and International Combines; other peoples cannot now come along and engage in industrial competition as though these stages had not been passed through.

No fiscal policy can prevent a people engaged in the world's competitive system from being directly affected by every evil attendant on that system, therefore it is that Australians must, not may, but must get far beyond the idea that Australia will build up a great Nation on the basis of competitive industry, and not be subjected to the social blight that is inseparable from that universal competition. But there is something much better than that in store for Australia. She will not be called upon to comply with the capitalists' demand of Cheap Labour and heavy product, or few wage receivers and much wool, timber, meat, dairy produce and minerals to export, to enable the capitalists to have big profits, not that, but better than that. Nor will Australia be called upon to comply with the demand made by many workers, and provide a 'living wage for all workers,' which she is not able to do now any more than either of the other competitive peoples. Not this, but much more than this. Australia is, in common with other countries, about to enter upon a period when industrial international competition will cease. The all-absorbing endeavour to supply every country with the products of every other country has been acted upon so successfully that it has already passed through the stages of relative success and failure, and is now decaying;

THE SUCCESS OF IT IS KILLING IT.

It was an excellent policy a century ago, it's coming to be a dead failure now. No country can now monopolise manufactures, or raw materials, or the fine arts; and the puny effects of preferential trade will at best mean nothing more than a trifling addition to the total demand of raw material from Australia. Competition has to be given up, and Cooperation will take its place, and Australian workmen and politicians must face the inevitable.

Again I repeat, Australia will not be built up on the basis of International industrial competition, no matter how many protective tariffs there may be, or how much scope may be afforded for the operation of free trade doctrines. I am not saying that fiscalism will not be necessary during the transition period, to enable industries to be built up and safe-guarded, the point I am seeking to make clear is this, that Australia's future depends upon the opportunities afforded to increasing numbers of people to provide the essentials of life for Australians on the highest and best scale, not by engaging in production for export, but in producing for Australian consumption. This does not in any sense forbid export of raw material in return for other material or commodities, where such is actually desired; but it changes the view-point, and changes the object, and therefore changes the policy.

The future of the world is to be Co-operative and not competitive, and Australia has an impossible task before her if there be no alternative but fighting for a share of the world's markets.

But there is an alternative, that of adequately supplying the needs of all who are here or care to come here; there is practically no limit to the population that could be maintained in the Australian Commonwealth, and on an ever advancing standard of well-being; but to do this all Legislative effort should be in the direction of National Co-operation.

Every Socialist man and woman, and every Labor man and woman should have as their watchword, NATIONAL CO-OPERATION. Therefore, as speedily as possible, the Land must be transferred to the Nation, the Industries must be taken over by the Nation, and the State i.e. the Nation must organise and run the industries including Scientific Agriculture, in the interests of the whole people Co-operatively.

Never had a people so glorious an opportunity to begin this as Australians now have. Even if America had desired to do it a century ago, in the then relatively infantile stage of economic development of the world it was impossible. Under Co-operation there can be no room for international hatreds and jealousies,

NO ROOM FOR ARMIES AND NAVIES FOR OFFENSIVE PURPOSES,

or to protect a sea-borne commerce against marauders; all this waste will absolutely cease, and the energy of every man will be welcomed and his reward will be sure.

Given a proper recognition of the stupendous advantages of National Co-operation, and right-away State Iron and Steel works would be started. Smelting works and Blast Furnaces, Rolling Mills and Engine Shops, and every encouragement would be given to every industry, the products of which made for general well-being. Under such conditions there would be no unemployed section, there never could be, there could be no poverty, there would therefore be no crime arising out of poverty. Would not this then be a country worth living in? And all this is realisable and that speedily; but we must face all it involves, and bid good-bye to international competitive industry, which is already tottering to its final fall. ... The Capitalists themselves know this full well and many, very many I believe, are glad to see the signs of the coming change. So with many of those officially connected with the Churches, I know a large number connected with religious denominations, who are sorely grieved at the grossly materialistic conditions that surround them and feel deeply the urgent necessity for a revolutionary change in the basis of human society, that change is at hand, but as yet only a minority are conscious of it, it is a change fraught with every blessing to mankind that the best amongst us could wish for. All hail the day, not distant now, when the mercenary spirit shall be replaced by that nobleness of nature all too lofty to be-mean itself or others by the mere pursuit of self.

APPENDIX

Considerable misunderstanding exists as to the annual value of production in the United Kingdom and Australia, and quite a number who quote Mr. Coghlan, are in utter confusion regarding 1st: Primary production; 2nd: Value of production from all Industries, and 3rd: Total income. Primary production, relates to Agricultural and Pastoral pursuits, Dairy Farming and Mining, and other primaries.

The table given by Coghlan in 'A Statistical Account of Australia and New Zealand' (1903–4) is taken from 'Mulhall's Dictionary of Statistics' for all countries except Australia, and is to be found on page 1021; and shows that Australia produces £89,144,000 per annum of primaries or £22 15s. 2d. per head of population per annum. The United Kingdom produces in primaries 317 millions of pounds or £7 18s. 6d. per head; France, £11 11s. 6d. per head; Germany, £8 13s. 4d.; United States, £14 14s. 0d.; Canada, £16 5s. 6d. These figures, however, give no indication at all as to the character of a Nation's welfare. As for instance with the United Kingdom, four-fifths of the Nation's work is on other than producing primaries, whilst in Australia the reverse is the case.

The value of the combined industries of Australia *i.e.* Manufactures in addition to primary products, amounted in 1903 to £117,672,000 or £30 0s. 10d. per head. See Coghlan's 'Statistical Account,' p. 1018.

This, however, does not give the total income of the people of the Commonwealth, as the services of many sections are called into requisition who, of course receive incomes, when all such services are included and allowed for, the income of the Australian Commonwealth amounts to £179,563,000 or £45 18s. 0d. per head. Mr. Coghlan gives no figures for countries outside Australia as to the value of the combined industries or the Total income; but the officially declared estimate of the Total income for the United Kingdom for 1903 is £1,750,000,000 (seventeen hundred and fifty millions of pounds) or £41 18s. 0d. per inhabitant.

CHAPTER FIVE

The War of the Classes*

On Sunday afternoon, 26 November 1905, I delivered the concluding address of a series held over several months on Sunday afternoons at the Gaiety Theatre, Melbourne. The subject of the address was The War of the Classes, being the title of Mr. Jack London's new book. Mr. London is an American, and the book referred to was published only a few months ago, and its purport is to demonstrate the existence of the Class War in America. It is a valuable production, most helpful to the student of Socialism, and I strongly recommend all who can to obtain a copy. The book is obtainable at the Tocsin Office, 23 Patrick Street, and from all Melbourne Booksellers.

On the following Saturday, 2 December, the *Age* published a special article on *The War of the Classes*, which is here printed verbatim. The same day I wrote a reply thereto and handed in the same to the *Age* office. . . . The reply, as sent to the *Age*, is also given, as, anticipating the *Age* would not publish such a reply, I kept a copy of it. The reply would have been longer and dealt with each point raised in the article but for consideration of the space required.

T.M.

The Article in *The Age*, of 2 December, 1905

THE WAR OF THE CLASSES

It might be expected that Mr. Tom Mann, after his experience as paid organiser of the Political Labour Council, would have found some definite, practical aims to work for. Instead of that he delivers lectures of only two sorts, neither of which has any useful bearing upon Australian labour problems. The first sort is that devoted to moonshiny suggestion, such as the adoption of a six hours' day by the employed to make work for the unemployed, or the proposal to nationalise the gold mines of Victoria, although it is a well-known fact

* First published by the Social Questions Committee, Melbourne, Dec. 1905.

that these are run at a loss. The other direction Mr. Mann breaks out into at intervals is a revival of the kind of Socialism which he might have heard when he was a small boy in London in the parks on Sunday afternoon. The split between the Socialists and the Anarchists occurred in 1872, and resulted in the formal expulsion of the latter in 1880. Yet at this time of day Mr. Mann thinks this rejected old Anarchistic raging good enough to rehash for the benefit of the Australian Labour party. His lecture of last Sunday on 'The War of the Classes' is the latest instance of his serving up in a half-warmed condition the curry that was too strong for the Socialists of even 25 years ago. Take an instance or two from last Sunday's harangue. We are solemnly assured 'It had been a curse of the English people that there had been an America and an Australia.' Here is all the incoherent contrariness of the old Anarchistic orations. The astonished reader, no doubt, wonders how Mr. Mann could have led up to such an extraordinary assertion. His own explanation is given in the following words: 'had there been no America and no Australia, there would have been a revolution in England before this.' So it appears that, as far as Mr. Mann is concerned, it would have been better if America and Australia had been blotted out, that England, with a fearfully crowded population, might have been precipitated into a revolution. This is so unreasonable that there is absolutely no danger in it. Meant for the growl of a man-eating tiger, it has only the effect of the spitting of a kitten.

Why should Australian labour be summoned together to listen to such nonsense? Mr. Mann has on more than one occasion outlined his own hare-brained schemes of communistic colonies in the bush, which are to absorb all the unemployed of Victoria, and especially of Melbourne. Yet, because America and Australia absorbed Britain's excess of population they are called by Mr. Mann the 'curse of England.' Perhaps it is actually against Mr. Mann's principles to do anything practical towards ameliorating the condition of labour in Australia, because any little improvements will only postpone the great social explosion, which to the Anarchistic variety of Socialist is the only thing worth living for. Yet it is instructive or amusing to follow the slender thread of Mr. Mann's thought a little farther back. He complains that America and Australia have spoiled the great English revolution that failed to arrive, because they absorbed the energetic and spirited elements of Britain's population, leaving the old country only the stale and flat drudges who have not enough kick in them to carry out a respectable revolution. One is inclined to wonder how Mr. Mann's confreres in the English Labour party will like this theory of the British workman, as a worm that has not sufficient strength to turn, or as beer so stale that it cannot send the cork flying and celebrate the event in an upheaval of revolutionary froth. But perhaps in England they know that Mr. Mann's strong point is not consistency, and that if for oratorical effect he gives English labour away on an Australian platform, he will make things even by adroitly depreciating Australian labour from an English platform when he returns to it. Meanwhile Mr. Mann has plainly recorded that his own personal ideal is revolutionary. All the modern Socialist leaders are careful to explain that they can rationally hope to reach their ideals only by evolution, and not at all by revolution. Mr. Mann's preference for the method of violence connects him with the crude minority that was expelled twenty-five years ago by the orderly Socialists. It would be interesting to learn how it came to pass that the Political Labour Council regarded this discredited and antiquated sort of doctrine as the suitable one on which to organise Victorian labour.

The very phrase, 'The War of the Classes,' which Mr. Mann took for the title of his last lecture, is borrowed from the early German Socialism, and is generally considered by the Socialistic leaders of the present day to embody one of the most serious of Marx's mistakes. The more advanced Socialistic ideal now is to promote the co-operation of the classes. It is frankly recognised that they do co-operate now, but that the process might go on much more efficiently if more rational and more moral ideals became prevalent. It is perfectly idle to speak of a war of the classes as long as every worker who gets an opportunity of becoming wealthy avails himself of it. If the owners of property were rightfully regarded as the enemies of the worker, it could not possibly happen that all the workers who got a chance of making money would abandon their class. The working man who has smart and capable sons never thinks that he is making war upon his own class when he struggles to educate them so that they can rise. Until that wonderful day arrives when the wise workman with a clever family impresses upon them all that it would be a sin for any of them to become richer than he was, this talk about the war of the classes is mere cant. It would be a terrible indictment of labour if all its best men deserted and went over to the hostile classes on the slightest chance. The Labour member of Parliament never insists that he shall take only so much salary as he could earn at his trade. It is perfectly futile then to lecture about the war of the classes as though it were an actual primary social fact, whereas such friction as exists between the classes is mostly a secondary product of human nature. It would be almost as reasonable to talk of the war between the trades because the raising of wages in one trade means a rise in the cost of its products when sold to the other trades as consumers. Between buyers and sellers there is always a sort of conflict of desires, but it would be a logical absurdity to assert that therefore all trade is a war. 'The War of the Classes' is a metaphor making for mischief, and ought to be dropped out of use in the discussion of social questions as long as the average individual does not feel it a personal sin to own more than his neighbours if he is able to do so.

The idea of the war of the classes has a good deal to do with another fundamental mistake of the Socialist extremists, namely, that labour creates all value. Misdirected labour creates only a nuisance. An amateur cobbler takes ten times as long to mend a pair of boots as a smart tradesman, and makes a bad job of the attempt too. It is nonsense to declare that by putting ten times the labour into the repairing he has turned out a piece of work ten times as valuable as the professional. Labour which makes things that are not wanted is simply wasted, and the reduction of this sort of waste is one of our real social problems. But these receive little attention from Mr. Mann when he is busy proclaiming his regrets that America and Australia ever existed because they have balked him of the fine English revolution which would have now been due if Australians and Americans were still cooped up in the old country.

Seeing that Mr. Tom Mann is the official lecturer of the Victorian Political Labour Council, it is time to inquire to what extent that body endorses the revolutionary teachings of its representative.

THE REPLY
to the preceding Article, as sent to The Age

To the Editor of The Age.

Sir, The article in to-day's issue, entitled 'The War of the Classes', deals with myself in so direct a fashion that I doubt not you will allow me to reply to the same.

I make no complaint of the criticisms passed upon me and upon what I have advocated, and what I am alleged to have advocated; but as the writer of the article is apparently under a misapprehension as to my connection with the Political Labour Council, I have to inform you that I am not now, and have not been for a year past, the 'official lecturer' of that body, so in fairness to the PLC I shall be glad if you will make the correction. I am a member of a branch of the PLC, but I occupy no official position whatever, and consequently that body cannot be responsible for anything I may advocate. Probably many of the members of the PLC are in agreement with me in what I advocate, and equally, probably, some are not in entire agreement. In any case, the lecture which is laid under criticism by the Age writer, delivered by me on Sunday last in the Gaiety Theatre, was given under the auspices of the 'Social Questions Committee,' of which I am the Organising Secretary.

The Age writer refers to my 'moonshiny' suggestion re a 'six hours' day,' and to my proposal to 'nationalise the gold mines of Victoria, although these are run at a loss.'

Briefly, as to the six hours' work day proposal, I have seriously advocated the necessity for a further reduction of working hours in Australia and all other countries. I have advised that before any attempt to secure a further reduction of working hours here be made, that negotiations be entered into with the workers of America and Europe, and, if possible, an agreement arrived at favourable to concerted action. Such a proposal carries all the necessary caution, and securely guards against indiscreet sectional or national attempts at limiting working hours.

Each country in turn has done something in the matter of reducing hours from the time when twelve hours per day was the all but universal rule, and the workers of every country testify to the fact that of all remedial agencies that have been resorted to for the purpose of improving the condition of the worker, none has been more potent for good than that of reducing the working hours; and no economist of any standing, no body of Social Reformers of intelligent repute, consider we have reached the limit of ameliorative effort in this direction. On the contrary, it is universally agreed that further changes in this direction must speedily take place. The ever increasing productivity of Labour renders this imperative.

As to the nationalisation of the mines of Victoria, the particular occasion when I dealt with that subject was an interview with an *Age* reporter who visited me by instruction of his superior to get my views on Socialism. I consented, and rattled off on the spot what commended itself to me as the correct principle and policy to suit the times. That interview appeared in the *Age* on 6 May 1904, and this is how I dealt with mining. Having made a definite proposal respecting an income tax, I said: 'Concurrently therewith we should proceed with the gradual taking over, or preparations for taking over, the coal mines in the State. We would impose a royalty upon the precious metals taken out of the State. This would give us not only the requisite income for all measures I have hinted at, but the necessary income to proceed with a gradual policy of State resumption of land. After resumption the land would not be sold, but let. If I were responsible I should, right away, undertake control of the mines. Knowing that we could not nationalise or socialise them, as yet, I should at once exercise State control over them, so that of all profits arising therefrom a certain percentage should be deducted for State purposes, for the further development of the mines. If that had been done to a reasonable extent during the life of this State, there would be enough wealth for the development of mines now lying idle.' I have no regrets or apologies to make for such proposals.

Respecting the title of the lecture criticised by the *Age*, 'War

of the Classes,' the *Age* writer displays a lack of knowledge of
the subject when he declares that this 'was too strong for the
Socialists of 25 years ago,' and has ever since been discarded.
Instead of this being true, the subject of my lecture was a
review of Jack London's latest book, entitled *War of the Classes*,
written by an American, and published, not 25 years ago, and
since discarded, but published in the year of grace 1905, and
now commanding a rapid sale in Collins-street, Melbourne.
The purport of the book is to describe the Class War as it now
literally obtains in that most successful of capitalistic countries,
the United States of America. The book is published for 2s. 6d.,
and I seize this opportunity to give it further publicity. Nothing
can be more educative to Victorians than that they should
know precisely the exploitation that is constantly going on in
Protectionist America, that they should know precisely the
degraded conditions under which millions of American
residents exist, and that they should know, with some
correctness, how bitterly the Class War is being waged there,
and know, also, what has led up to it. Mr. London's book
enables one to understand this, and a wonderful eye-opener it
is. The book absolutely demonstrates not only the existence of
the Class War in America, but shows that its nature and
meaning is clearly understood. Last year 435,000 Socialist votes
were recorded for the Socialist candidate for the Presidency of
the USA, an increase of nearly 400 per cent in four years. 'Ah,'
it may be asked, 'but what kind of Socialism?' This is the
American's up-to-date reply, not the European's of 25 years
ago. Says Mr. London:

It is its (Socialism) purpose to wipe out, root and branch, all
capitalistic institutions of present-day society. It is distinctly
revolutionary, and in scope and depth is vastly more tremendous than
any revolution that has ever occurred in the history of the world. It
presents a new spectacle to the astonished world, that of an *organised,
international, revolutionary movement.*

Says the *Age* critic: 'It is perfectly idle to speak of a War of the
Classes as long as every worker who gets an opportunity of
becoming wealthy avails himself of it.' Mr. London deals with
this subject for his country, and shows clearly that so long as
the capable young men in the working class could lift
themselves out of that class and join the exploiters, they did so
with alacrity; but now the doors are closed. 'Rockefeller has
shut the door on oil, the American Tobacco Company on
tobacco, and Carnegie on steel. After Carnegie came Morgan,
who triple locked the door. These doors will not open again,

and before them pause thousands of ambitious young men to read the placard, "No THOROUGHFARE." And day by day more doors are shut, while the ambitious young men continue to be born. It is they, denied the opportunity to rise from the Working Class, who preach revolt to the Working Class.'

The capitalists are shrewd enough to know that an outlet for such young men must be afforded, or internal social revolt will receive attention; and it is here that my remarks hold true upon the effects on English Working Class life that the opening up of America and Australia has had. When the energetic and capable young fellows at Home began to show signs of deep-seated uneasiness, what better could the monopolists do than advise, through their specially devised agencies, that in the newer world there was ample scope for all – at one time America, at another Australia, and later South Africa – always with the two-fold object of finding an outlet for energy which would be sure to make itself felt one way or another, and at the same time to develop new markets for further capitalist exploitation.

Even in Victoria after the boom period of a dozen years ago, many a demand would have been formulated and enforced had not Western Australia afforded scope for pent-up energy. Therefore it is that we Socialists rejoice that Empire building is drawing to a close. Empires exist not in the true interests of the whole people, but to enable a class to perpetuate its domination.

Says the *Age* writer again: '"The War of the Classes" is a metaphor making for mischief, and ought to be dropped out of use in the discussion of social questions.' We know full well it isn't pleasant for the plutocracy to hear the naked truth set forth; but seeing that Socialists do not consider it necessary to propitiate the exploiting class, and are desirous of educating the workers, honesty of expression accompanies honesty of conviction, and although my critic claims to know what Socialists do and do not advocate, I may be permitted to direct attention to the view of revolution held by Socialists. The *Age* writer may be excused for not being well posted in a subject not by any means his own. Anyone to read to-day's article and stop at that would be seriously misled. Says the *Age*: 'All the modern Socialist leaders are careful to explain that they can rationally hope to reach their ideals only be evolution, and not at all by revolution.' This from a non-Socialist. Now from a representative Socialist who has been in the English movement from its inception until this hour, Mr. H. M. Hyndman, of the

English Social Democratic Federation, whose voice and pen have been persistently used for the past twenty-three years in the advocacy of Socialism. On page 4 of Mr. Hyndman's volume on 'The Economics of Socialism' is the following: 'Those who try to draw a distinction between evolution and revolution, or speak of evolutionary and revolutionary Socialism and Socialists, misunderstand the entire theory of sociological development as formulated by the whole scientific school. Revolution simply means that the evolution of society has reached the point where a complete transformation, both external and internal, has become immediately inevitable. No man, and no body of men, can make such a revolution before the time is ripe for it, though, as men become conscious instead of unconscious agents in the development of the society in which they live, and of which they form a part, they may themselves help to bring about this revolution peaceably instead of by violence. A successful revolution, whether effected in the one way or the other, merely gives legal expression and sanction to the new forms, which, for the most part unobserved or disregarded, have developed in the womb of the old society.'

Into the merits of the *Age* paragraph dealing with 'misdirected labour creating a nuisance instead of value,' this is of so erudite a character that I let it pass; but I urge upon Victorians the necessity of studying Socialism. If it is wrong, reject it; but do not, for shame's sake, allow the human suffering to continue without an honest effort to understand its cause and to find a cure.

TOM MANN,
Secretary Social Questions Committee

Collins-street, 2 December 1905

CHAPTER SIX

The Way to Win

An Open Letter to Trades Unionists on
*Methods of Industrial Organisation**

Comrades, The great crisis is drawing nigh when the supreme effort must be made by the workers to take entire responsibility for the management of all industry and commerce; the existing system of society must of necessity give place to some other system that will adequately provide for the requirements of all.

The nature of the newer order will depend in considerable measure on the standard of intelligence possessed by the workers, and their courage to apply sound principles that will ensure social and economic equality.

The object I have in writing this letter is not to enlarge upon principles or ideals, but to direct attention to the machinery that is necessary to enable us to achieve our object.

THE PRELIMINARY ESSENTIAL CONDITION IS WORKING-CLASS SOLIDARITY

Without this solidarity, i.e., without the power and the disposition to act in concert as the working-class against the dominating plutocratic class, there is no hope.

At present we have not got this solidarity, either industrially or politically.

The weakness of our industrial organisation lies less in the fact that only one-fourth of the workers are organised, than in the much more serious fact that those who are organised are not prepared to make common cause with each other.

Hitherto we have been content with trades unions – meaning unions of skilled workers, supplemented by unions of unskilled workers. But each of these unions has for the most part initiated and as far as possible carried out a policy for itself alone; more recently broadened out somewhat by joining Trade and Labor Federations to secure something in the nature of general help in time of trouble or warfare.

* First published by 'Barrier Daily Truth,' Broken Hill, May 1909.

Still, the basis of unionism to-day is distinctly sectional and narrow, instead of cosmopolitan and broad-based.

In Australia, more particularly, resort to Arbitration Courts and Wages Boards for the settlement of industrial disputes has resulted in settlements being arrived at and agreements entered into by the various unions, binding them not to become actively engaged in any dispute during the period covered by the agreement.

Such agreements in themselves absolutely destroy the possibility of class solidarity.

Agreements entered into between unions and employers directly – i.e., without the intervention of Arbitration Courts or Wages Boards – are equally detrimental to, and in dead opposition to working-class solidarity. They, therefore, must be classed as amongst the chief obstructive agencies to general working-class progress.

Thus it is clear that to continue entering into binding agreements with employers is to render the unionist movement impotent for achieving our economic freedom.

Therefore, no more agreements must be entered into for lengthy periods. Of course, temporary adjustments must be made, but they must be for the hour only, leaving the workers free for concerted action with their fellows.

The form of capitalist industry has changed during the past 50 years. It has passed through the stages of individual ownership of shop or factory, the employer taking part in the business and competing with all other employers in the same business, then to limited liability and joint stock companies, which removed the individual employer – whose place is taken by a manager – and reduced competition between the capitalist firms. From this it has now gone to trusts and combines, inter-State, and even international in their operation.

A corresponding progress must take place with the workers' organisation. Sectionalism must disappear, and the industrial organisations must be equal to State, national, and international action, not in theory only, but in actual fact.

Another influence tending strongly towards discord and not towards solidarity, is the stipulating in some unions that a man who joins an industrial organisation by that act pledges himself to vote in a certain way politically.

I have, in days gone by, argued strongly that the industrial organisations should be the special places where economic knowledge should be imparted and adequate scope for discussion afforded. I hold so still, but I am thoroughly satisfied that it is a source of serious discord to couple the political with the industrial in the sense of demanding that a man must vote as the industrial organisation declares.

It is not difficult to understand why this should be so. It is because in the unions or industrial organisations we are (or should be) prepared to enrol every person who works, irrespective of his or her intelligence, or opinions held upon political or other subjects.

Take the case of an organiser, who finds himself in a centre of industry where there is practically no organisation. He soon discovers that the usual orthodox bodies are there, theological and political. He finds out the composition of the local governing bodies and the type of politician who received the votes at last election. From this he concludes that there are resident there the usual percentage of reactionaries, Liberals, Laborites, and Socialists, and each of these parties finds its adherents chiefly in the ranks of the workers.

That ought not to interfere with industrial organisation, in which they should be enrolled entirely irrespective of political faith; and becoming members of the industrial body, it is here these workers should get their education in industrial and social economics, and this would prove the true guide to political action.

To insist upon them voting solidly politically before they have received instruction in matters economic, is to add to the difficulties of organisation.

Notwithstanding what has been done and is now being done by the Australian Workers' Union, it is abundantly clear that we shall have to separate the industrial from the political, and so afford scope for growing activities with the least amount of friction.

I am not wishful to deprecate political action, but it is necessary to say that during recent years, in Australia, undue importance has been attached to political action; and although the actual membership in industrial organisations may be as large, or even larger than in former years, there is not held by the typical unionist a proper understanding of the fundamental and vital importance of economic or industrial organisation. Indeed, to listen to the speeches of the typical Labor politician it is clear that he is surfeited with the idea that that which is of paramount importance is the return to the legislative bodies of an additional number of Labor men, and that all else is secondary and relatively trifling.

In absolute fact, the very opposite is the case. Experience in all countries shows most conclusively that industrial organisation, intelligently conducted, is of much more moment than political action, *for entirely irrespective as to which school of politicians is in power, capable and courageous industrial activity forces from the politicians proportionate concessions.*

It is an entirely mistaken notion to suppose that the return of Labor men or Socialists to Parliament can bring about deep-seated economic changes, unless the people themselves intelligently desire these changes, and those who do so desire know the value of economic organisation. During the past few years the representative men of France, Germany, Italy, and other countries have urged upon the workers of the world to give increased attention to industrial organisation, and they are acting accordingly.

Indeed, it is obvious that a growing proportion of the intelligent pioneers of economic changes are expressing more and more dissatisfaction with Parliament and all its works, and look forward to the time when Parliaments, as we know them, will be superceded by the people managing their own affairs by means of the Initiative and the Referendum.

However, I am not an anti-Parliamentarian. I am chiefly concerned that we should attend to the first job in the right order, and thus make it the easier to do whatever else may be necessary.

It is encouraging to see the practical turn of affairs in Port Pirie, SA. There the Combined Unions' Committee has already sent out a circular letter to the unions of South Australia, in which they say:

During the present struggle with the Broken Hill Proprietary Company, we have had ample opportunity of ascertaining in what manner industrial organisation might be made more effective in resisting the tyrannical encroachments of modern capitalism, and securing to the worker a larger share of the product of his labor. My Committee have come to a definite and unanimous conclusion that craft unionism has outlived its usefulness, and that 20th century industrial development demands on the part of the workers a more perfect system of organisation. With this end in view we urge, as a preliminary step, the holding of a Trades' Union Congress in Adelaide during the month of July next. We sincerely hope that this proposition will meet with the earnest and energetic support of your members, and that immediate action will be taken.

This is a significant sign of the times, and an encouraging one, too, to those who lament the sectionalism of the present unionism movement.

Such a conference could well discuss and carry such resolutions as follow:

That the present system of sectional trades unionism is incapable of combatting effectively the capitalist system under which the civilised world is now suffering, and such modifications and alterations should be made in the existing unions as will admit of a genuine Federation of all organisations, with power to act unitedly for industrial purposes.

That this Conference urgently advises all trade societies, unions, and associations to speedily make such changes in their rules as may be necessary to separate the funds subscribed for purposes usually provided by Friendly Societies from the funds subscribed for economic or industrial purposes, and proceed to at once form district Federations of all unions as distinct from trade or craft Federations.

That a Provisional Committee, or Council, be formed in each State (or, if need be, in each industrial district), to direct organising activities, until the movement attains such dimensions as will warrant the holding of an Interstate Congress, at which Congress all details as to objects and methods can be definitely decided upon. The members composing such provisional councils or committees to be drawn from members of unions agreeing to the previous proposals.

That no dispute be entered upon and no encouragement given to any section to formulate grievances (unless compelled by the action of employers), until the movement shall have attained a high standard of organisation, approved by the proposed Interstate Congress.

That in order to guard against dissension, it be declared from the outset that this movement is neither anti-political nor pro-political, but industrial and economic, and that members may belong to what political organisation they please providing they do not oppose the expressed objects and ideals yet to be agreed upon at the Inter-state Congress, and at present set forth in the previous proposals.

If the unions of the Barrier agree to take such action as suggested in the foregoing proposals, I believe there could be, in a short time, a far more powerful organisation than anything of the kind known to modern times.

Beyond any question, the industrialists of Australia are prepared to carefully consider any well thought-out proposals submitted to them by the comrades of Broken Hill and Port Pirie.

The time is particularly opportune also, because for some two years past much discussion has been indulged in as to the merits of industrial unionism, and the minds of many are prepared to co-operate in such effort as here set forth.

Many of the unions in New South Wales and Victoria have already given much attention to the subject, and are well disposed thereto.

To remain in the present forcibly feeble condition

characteristic of present-day unionism would be to stamp ourselves as incapables; and would admit of an indefinite prolongation of capitalist tyranny.

On all sides we see hysterical efforts being made by the plutocratic Governments of the different countries to prepare for war on an unprecedented scale, as a relief from glutted markets. Such is the condition of the peoples in Europe and America that deaths by starvation and deaths from diseases arising out of ill-nourished and unsanitary conditions are so appallingly large that the modern system stands condemned in the eyes of all intelligent citizens.

Through the ages men have died by millions before the naturally allotted span of life, because they have not been able to produce life's requirements in the necessary abundance; but never before did the anomaly we now witness obtain, viz., that people die of hunger because they have produced so much as to glut the markets and fill the warehouses, and are then deprived of the opportunity of work, therefore of incomes. Hence, poverty, destitution, and misery.

These conditions cannot last. In spite of colossal ignorance, there is already too much intelligence and genuine courage to acquiesce in such class dominancy and exploitation as bring such results in its train.

Therefore, comrades, get to work like men of intelligence and courage, count it a privilege to be permitted to share in the great work of social and economic emancipation; for, indeed, there is no higher, no worthier, no holier work that can engage the energies of man.

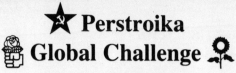

★ Perstroika
Global Challenge ✿

Our Common Future

edited by Ken Coates

A serious crisis of the environment has assumed the proportions of a global menace. This has been pinpointed by the UN Commission headed by Mrs Brundtland, the Norwegian Prime Minister, whose report, *Our Common Future*, was published last year.

The Global Challenge involved in this crisis is aggravated in the economic crisis of monetarism and debt, brilliantly analysed in the programme of the Socialist International.

Now Mikhail Gorbachev has addressed the same themes in a powerful message to the United Nations. The power of separate nation states is now insufficient to meet this world-wide threat. Can the peoples join their forces to prepare joint international action on the necessary scale?

This is the agenda of this important book featuring contributions by Mikhail Gorbachev, Michael Barratt Brown, Keith and Anne Buchanan, Luciana Castellina, Ken Coates, Andre Gunder Frank, Stuart Holland, Bob de Ruiter, Marek Thee, Marten van Traa, Joop den Uyl, Norbert Wieczorek,
It is introduced by Neil Kinnock.

"Should command attention and be widely discussed"
Neil Kinnock

"We can speak till we are blue in the face . . . Nothing will change till we start acting"
Mikhail Gorbachev

Cloth £17.50 Paper £4.95
from Spokesman, Bertrand Russell House, Gamble Street, Nottingham NG7 4ET

Spreading the News
by Frank Allaun

The next few years will be a crucial time for the British media. In television and radio, the advent of satellite and cable broadcasting continued with the present government's 'free market' policies could lead to a drastic lowering of standards in an industry which has attracted world acclaim.

In the press, the technological revolution *could* lead to a reverse of today's stranglehold by just five huge press groups. But, those powerful proprietors are also major shareholders in TV and radio companies.

Frank Allaun, for many years a distinguished politician who made reform of the media one of his principal concerns, and before that a successful journalist, surveys the state of both press and broadcasting and explores the opportunities and dangers that now present themselves.

**120pp 210 × 140mm
cloth 0 85124 488 2 £17.50
paper 0 85124 498 X £4.95**

The Life of John Wheatley
by John Hannan

John Wheatley was the architect of left-wing opposition on Red Clydeside during the First World War. He alone commanded the loyalty and respect of all the different groupings amongst the socialists including such diverse firebrands as Maxton, Gallagher and Kirkwood.

Wheatley subsequently became a Minister in the 1924 Labour Government, his Housing Act becoming the one lasting monument of that administration. His challenge to the British Labour movement after its fall remains pertinent today.

**208pp 210 × 140mm
cloth 0 85124 487 4 £17.50
paper 0 85124 497 1 £5.95**

Idle Hands, Clenched Fists:
The Depression in a Shipyard Town

by Stephen Kelly

There were people watching the Toxteth riots of 1981 who had seen it all before. In the Autumn of 1932, those on the dole in Birkenhead had reacted similarly, venting their anger against the police as their frustration finally reached breaking point. Many stories of those earlier riots have been passed down by word of mouth, but little that is accurate has actually been written about them. This book, for the first time, records in detail the events of that Autumn on Merseyside.

106pp 210 × 140mm
cloth 0 85124 436 X £15.00
paper 0 85124 446 7 £4.95

Hanging on by your Fingernails:
The Struggle at Lea Hall 1984-87

Photographs and design: Nigel Dickinson
Text: Jon Williams & Liliane Jaddou

From almost the start of the Strike at Lea Hall Colliery, Nigel Dickinson began taking photographs which were exhibited on the walls of the Strike Centre, or regularly passed round and discussed. They came not only to represent a collective point of view, but to help build that point of view.

By the end of the strike there was a photographic record which was perhaps unique in Labour Movement History. 151 photographs from it are published in this book together with a commentary produced in much the same way as the photographs, under the ultimate editorial control of those who had been involved in the Strike.

56pp A4
paper 0 85124 486 6 £4.25

Cooperatives that work
New Constitutions, Conversions and Tax
by Paddy Smith

There is an increasing interest in measures which can enable worker cooperatives to expand in size and number and to become a significant sector of the economy. This book, written by lawyers, explores in detail how workers' control can be dovetailed into mainstream financial and legal business arrangements without sacrificing the basic principles of the cooperative movement. As the first guide to show how company and tax law and practice can be used in this way, it is an invaluable source of advice to all would-be cooperators and their sponsors.

**180pp approx 210 × 140mm
cloth 0 85124 452 1 £25.00
paper 0 85124 462 9 £8.95**

Wales in Closed
by Ralph Fevre

As the job losses gathered pace, the graffiti on the Severn Bridge announced that "Wales is Closed". But it is not just the drastic reduction in *volume* of employment that has had such a devastating effect on the workforce of the steel industry. Insecurity and *under*employment through the mechanism of casual or temporary work with private contractors are now conditions necessary to the production of steel. In the Port Talbot steelworks since 1980, the author traces what might be called the quiet privatisation of British Steel.

**164pp 210 × 140mm
cloth 0 85124 466 1 £17.50
paper 0 85124 476 9 £5.95**

Britain's Regions in Crisis No. 4

A Putney Plot

by Peter Hain

In 1975/6, Peter Hain was arrested and tried at the Old Bailey for a bank robbery which he had not committed. At the time, public allegations of a South African plot (as result of Hain's activism against Apartheid) could not be substantiated. But since then evidence has come to light, including revelations by Peter Wright, the former MI5 agent, which lend support to those allegations.

This book re-opens the argument. The first part covers the arrest and trial; the second asks whether Hain's case was part of a much bigger and more sinister political attack from the Far Right, working through the intelligence services.

180pp 210 × 140mm
cloth 0 85124 471 8 £19.95
paper 0 85124 481 5 £5.95

Pigs' Meat:
Selected Writings of Thomas Spence

Ed. G. I. Gallop

In the Story of the emergence of British radicalism and socialism in the late 18th and early 19th century, the works of Thomas Spence are an indispensable element.

192pp 210 × 140mm
cloth 0 85124 315 0 £35.00
paper 0 85124 424 6 £5.95